BAD MANNERS
Driving Your Clients
CRAZY ?

FIND OUT HOW & **FIX IT** NOW!

---

by Stephanie Horton

Author's Photo:
Fay Marley-Clarke, Photographer, Artist
www.FayMarley-Clarke.com

Layout / Design:
Carl & Laurie Berg
www.TheGraphicsRanch.com

First Edition

ISBN: 978-0-6152-0162-7

www.topdogetiquette.com

Introducing . . .

Stephanie Rowland Horton
Top Dog Etiquette, LLC

Known as "The Common Courtesy Coach," Stephanie Horton is a professional speaker and author who educates business professionals in world class etiquette and manners. She prides herself in helping people develop rewarding business relationships through the power of common courtesy. From slurping oysters to saving yourself from especially embarrassing moments at cocktail parties and dinners, Stephanie Horton's energetic presentations and entertaining etiquette tips are popular among business and social organizations alike.

Stephanie Horton is a certified international etiquette consultant from The Protocol School of Washington, D.C., a University of Washington broadcast journalism graduate with 25 years' experience in communications and hospitality, and is also a Certified Meetings Professional, "CMP." She is also the creator/instructor of Highline Community College's Event Management Certificate Program. Her first book, "Full House: Selling Rooms and Space with Style and Grace" has been enthusiastically received by the hospitality community.

Prior to starting her career as a professional speaker in 1996, Stephanie worked in television news, meeting management, hotel sales and service, credit union and forest industry marketing and communications. She was born in Tacoma, Washington, was a 1972 graduate of Curtis High School (remember Stephanie Rowland?) and enjoys the Pacific Northwest to its fullest from her home on the Puget Sound in Washington. Let the oyster slurping begin . . .

For more information on booking Stephanie Horton for your next event, visit www.topdogetiquette.com, or call her at (360) 275-7370.

— *Thank you* —

I am honored to dedicate this book to my parents,
Audrey and Chuck Rowland, and to my brothers,
Randy Rowland, Ph.D and Michael Rowland.

Thanks to them, my life has always been
a safe and happy place, where I have felt loved,
valued, and respected. They have taught me,
by example, how to treat others
with respect and dignity. Thank you.

Are Bad Manners Driving Your Clients Crazy?

by Stephanie Horton

— Part One —

INTRODUCTION 11

Chapter 1 – A Lighthearted Look at Useful Etiquette. 13
Mad Manners: from Bad to Beautiful! and The Kind Mind

Chapter 2 – Getting Started — Making All People Feel Comfortable! 17
That Means Everybody and What's the Big Deal

— Part Two —

GREETING PEOPLE WITH STYLE AND GRACE 19

Chapter 3 – Handshaking and Introductions Made Easy (Business and Social) . . 21
Introductions. Do It. and Meeting People with Disabilities

Chapter 4 – Extra Touches – Hugging and Business Cards 31
Hugging: Avoid It! and Business Card Protocol

— Part Three —

CONVERSATION ETIQUETTE 35

Chapter 5 – Business Conversation. 37
*Getting Personal, The Ultimate Bore, Language, Taking Notes at the Table
and Table-Hopping*

— Part Four —

MEETING MANNERS 43

Chapter 6 – Impromptu and Scheduled Meetings 45
Impromptu Meetings and Scheduled Meetings

Chapter 7 – Meeting over Cocktails and Meals. 49
Breakfast and Luncheon Meetings, Cocktail and Dinner Meetings

— *Part Five* —

THE ART OF DINING 53

Chapter 8 – The Big Picture - Are you the Host or Guest? 55

Chapter 9 – Dining Details 61
Napkins Please! Ordering Food and Beverages, About Alcohol, Understanding the Table Setting, Handling the Knife and Fork, The "Resting" Position, Silverware Tips, Eating Soup, Dessert

Chapter 10 – At the Table–Things to Keep in Mind 69
Seating, Purse Placement, Sneezing and Nose Blowing, Where to Put your Hands, How to Hold Glasses, Thanking the Servers

— *Part Six* —

ATTENDING CONVENTIONS & SPECIAL EVENTS 75

Chapter 11 — What is your Objective? 77

Chapter 12 — Taking Convention Guests for a Meal 81

Chapter 13 — Tips on Tipping 85
Fine Dining, Fast Food Delivery, Hotels, Taxis and Limousines, and Airport

— *Part Seven* —

CORPORATE SPECIAL EVENTS 89

Chapter 14 — Prepare and Participate! 91

Chapter 15 — Dancing Etiquette 93

Chapter 16 — Golf Etiquette 95

— *Part Eight* —

OFFICE ETIQUETTE. 101

Chapter 17 — Professional Manners: Where do you stand? 105
Office Behavior Check-Up, What is your word usage saying about you?, Office Gift Giving: Who cares? Personal Cell Phones, Office Chat, Should Women Open Doors for Men? Elevator Etiquette - Yes!

Chapter 18 — Internationally Speaking 115

— *Part Nine* —

HIGH TECH ETIQUETTE TUNE-UP. 119

Chapter 19 — Telephone and Cell Phone Etiquette 121

Chapter 20 — E-mail Etiquette 125

— *Part Ten* —

LOOKING THE PART 129

Chapter 21 — Business Casual Confusion 131

— *Part Eleven* —

PERSONALLY SPEAKING 137

Chapter 22 — Remembering the Social Graces 139
Dating, Alcohol Alert, Attending Celebrations and Family Events, House Guests, Managing Awkward Moments

Chapter 23 — It's High Time for Afternoon Tea 147
Invitations, Table Setting, Tea, Food & Music, Role of the Hostess, How to Properly Drink Tea

— *Part Twelve* —

POLISHING THE APPLE 151

Chapter 24 — A Little Polish Goes a Long Way 153
   Gender, Door Opening, Business Clothing, Paying the Check, Flirting, Kissing, Gum,
   Public Displays of Affection (PDA), One more thing

—— APPENDIX ——
How to eat certain foods
Place setting maps, formal and informal

— *Part One* —
INTRODUCTION

If you are nervous before introducing your boss to a new client, find yourself confused by multiple knives and forks at a dinner party, or wonder why you keep getting passed over for promotions or second dates, this book is for you. Business and personal relationships alike take attention and dedication, and it all begins with how we treat one another. From that first handshake to a thank-you note, how do your manners measure up?

Do you feel like running the other way when the topic of "etiquette" is mentioned? If so, you are not alone. Many people are overwhelmed by the topic and the "rules" it implies we should already know. The fact is that many people do *not* know the rules (I prefer calling them guidelines) of manners. When I make presentations to groups, people often wait to talk to me about how the topic of manners was handled in their particular lives, and I always find it interesting. Some people have had the luxury of parents who taught them everything from how to eat soup to handshaking and introductions.

> *There are risks and costs to a program of action.*
> *But they are far less than the long range risks*
> *and costs of comfortable inaction. –John F. Kennedy*

Others had no such training. The bottom line is that learning and practicing good manners is a life-long journey, and the more we can learn along the way, the more we will enjoy the confidence that comes with that education – both professionally and personally.

Over the past ten years I have noticed that most of my clients have one thing in common: whether a business executive, college student or parent endeavoring to teach good manners to a child, *confusion* seems to be the common bond that brings us to the etiquette table to learn! So rest easy, because this short guide is designed to give you the basics in a quick read. This book will set the stage for *confidence*, not *confusion*, when it comes to your manners – at work, at home, and at play.

Could bad manners be driving people crazy?

The only way I could find out was to ask, so I did! Let's just say, "WOW!" – I learned what bothers people in a major way. Look for the **"Here's what's driving people crazy"** box at the beginning of each section. One idea would be to use these gems as topics for a staff meeting or retreat. They provide some entertaining food for thought!

Here's what's driving people crazy –

1. People think the rules of good manners apply to everyone else, not them.

2. My boss treats me too informally, especially in front of clients.

3. People don't pronounce my name correctly.

4. My guest is ignored at business/social dinners.

5. I am ignored when I arrive at a meeting or party.

— Chapter 1 —
A Lighthearted Look at Useful Etiquette

MAD MANNERS: FROM BAD TO BEAUTIFUL!

I know that most of us have been taught to have *good*, not *bad* manners, but what's this *mad* manners all about? It is very simple. **Bad manners drive people crazy.** The number one comment I receive from anyone at my talks, whether a private corporate setting or a large convention, always starts with "it drives me crazy when . . ." followed by etiquette pet peeves that people can't WAIT to tell me. Bad manners drive people mad!

So how do we deal with this dilemma? Turn bad manners into beautiful manners, and you're all set. It's the easiest way to think about it. If you can think about your behaviors and mannerisms as being perceived as "beautiful" by others, you are well on your way to turning the corner to appropriate professional and personal presence.

I like to use the word "beautiful" because it helps us define both our presence and our behaviors and also helps us figure out what to do! Is it *beautiful* to chew with your mouth open? Is it *beautiful* to sneeze into your napkin? I'm sure you get the picture. By asking yourself if what you are about to say or do would be considered "beautiful," you may have answered your own etiquette dilemma!

Most people agree that good manners are a matter of common sense, generally speaking, but appreciate a few reminders when it comes to the details of meeting and greeting, dining and dating. And, unfortunately, some people forget that good manners are appreciated personally as well as professionally. Whether you're attending a football game with clients or friends, your social graces can make the difference between a mediocre time or a great time when all is said and done. Did your cell phone interrupt conversation during the game? Did you monopolize the conversation and not allow anyone else to join in? Did you drop off your guests at the door where it is cozy and warm? Make no mistake, buying the tickets or extending an invitation is just the beginning!

Throughout this book I will use "professional and personal" almost interchangeably as I discuss appropriate manners and behavior because I believe it is just as important to treat people with dignity and respect at home as it is in the workplace. And, of course — practice makes perfect. If we practice these behaviors throughout all aspects of our lives, then we never have to worry. Beautiful manners will become second nature, and you will never have to worry about driving people crazy!

THE KIND MIND

Let's begin by thinking about how we approach certain life situations. Have you ever wondered why you have been passed over for promotions or special projects? Or perhaps why your best friend has more fun at parties than you do?

If you've ever felt left out and wondered why, it might be time to rethink the way you approach others. It's true that people prefer to work – and play — with people they like, which makes us wonder – "do people enjoy being around me?"

In business relationships, business doesn't make deals, people do, and that means building long-term business relationships. The same is true for personal business! It starts with the basics of business etiquette – a warm, welcoming smile; a hearty, meaningful handshake; making others feel valued, comfortable, and at ease no matter what the surroundings. I call it "the kind mind" attitude. People will find it a joy to be around you. How?

When you have a "kind mind," you put people first. By *assuming* the best and *expecting* the best from others, you are more likely to *get* the best – from yourself and others – by treating everyone with the same level of respect and courtesy.

A leader with a kind mind at work exhibits a seemingly effortless sense of grace and style. He or she understands how to honor other people by introducing them correctly, toasting at the appropriate times, or choosing an appropriate hostess gift. Unfortunately, in our culture these basic elements of the social graces are often overlooked. A mispronounced name, inappropriate language or conversation, or overlooked RSVP are all culprits in our fast-paced world, leaving hurt feelings and bungled business deals in their wake. The irony is that the offending parties often never know the real reason behind the resulting "cold shoulder," as that would be a breach of etiquette rule No. 1 – "never embarrass anyone!"

The *kind mind* is a way of life, a realization that when the priority is placed on people, the results are always positive. Sometimes we have to step out of our comfort zones when it comes to putting the "kind mind" concept into action. No more hiding in the produce section at the grocery store to escape saying hello to your boss or an old friend!

— Chapter 2 —
Getting Started
Making All People Feel Comfortable!

THAT MEANS EVERYBODY!

Now that you understand the concepts of beautiful manners and the kind mind, let's get started. As I am fond of mentioning often, there really *is* a magic formula when it comes to beautiful manners: A person with beautiful manners sees to it that everyone is ALWAYS comfortable and that they are NEVER embarrassed. Sounds easy, right? It can be!

When I say "everyone," that is exactly what I mean. From young to old, new acquaintances to old friends, women to men, make sure you treat ALL people the same – and make them comfortable, both physically and emotionally. How do we accomplish this? In general, greet them with a warm smile and solid handshake, introduce them to other people, and offer them a seat and a beverage. More? hang up their coats, explain the schedule of the day, where the restrooms are, etc. All of these things will help make others feel welcome and comfortable.

When it comes to embarrassing people, it is a bit more complex. Ask yourself, "Is what I am about to say or do apt to embarrass this person?" If so, stop dead in your tracks and think through how your comment or behavior might affect *everyone* at the table or conversation circle. Keep in mind that our personalities differ. For example, I would not be particularly embarrassed to be made fun of if I spilled a drink or dropped a napkin ring in my coffee (yes, it happened). Some people would be very embarrassed, and perhaps even offended to be made fun of in this way.

I once had someone tell me – in great detail – the story of a flying steak at a dinner party. It seemed that her knife slipped when she was attempting to cut her meat, and the entire steak flew across the table onto the floor. Then the floodgates of teasing started and continued throughout the entire evening. No big deal? The person telling me the story was now in her seventies. This happened to her at her sixteenth birthday party – *and she was horrified.*

Possessing beautiful manners means that you think ahead to avoid pitfalls like this. The Big question is: "How will my behavior affect everyone else? Remember, a joke may not be funny to everyone, so tread lightly when it comes to comedy!

> *When bad manners turn people off or drive them crazy they will not tell you because that would be equally rude and most likely embarrass you.*

WHAT'S THE BIG DEAL?

I cannot move on without mentioning the flip side – what happens if you do happen to make people uncomfortable or embarrass them. Some people have actually said to me when explaining some guffaw they made, "It was no big deal! They didn't even mention it!" And to that I think to myself a resounding "hmmmm . . . wonder why." It's true that they would never tell you – for fear of embarrassing YOU! So you will never know. It might be a missed business opportunity (they simply will never call you back). Or it might be that second date you never had.

— *Part Two* —
GREETING PEOPLE
WITH STYLE AND GRACE

If you think all eyes are on you when you enter a room, you are most likely correct! It is human nature to constantly observe our surroundings and the people around us, so this is the perfect opportunity to show off your social skills and make a fabulous first impression. Take a deep breath, smile, and walk into the room like you are supposed to be there (you are!) – and prepare to smile and shake hands. Stand tall and proud, look people in the eye, and genuinely *listen* to them, and you will be a hit!

Remember that most people feel a bit uneasy when attending events and receptions. Your welcoming greeting and interesting conversation will be most appreciated.

> *Human beings, like plants, grow in the soil of acceptance,*
> *not in the atmosphere of rejection.* — *John Powell, S.J.*

Here's what's driving people crazy –

1. People hold too much of a stare or gaze inappropriately at parts of my body.

2. People shake my hand so hard it hurts!

3. People call me by my first name when we have never met. Or, they immediately call me by a nickname when they don't even know me.

4. Business contacts hug me — not only at business events, but at social events as well.

5. People are unaware that their hugging may actually hurt people who have had surgery or medical issues.

6. Group lunch attendees pass their cards around a table before they have actually met their other tablemates.

7. Business contacts write on my business card in front of me.

— *Chapter 3* —
Handshaking and Introductions
Made Easy *(Business and Social)*

HANDSHAKING. DO IT.

Have you ever experienced someone else's poor handshake? Perhaps the ever-popular "limp" connection that leaves you feeling uncomfortable? Handshaking is important – period. While handshaking is acceptable in most countries, some countries do have their own forms of greeting, such as bowing in Japan. In the United States, handshaking is our form of greeting.

The purpose of a handshake is to demonstrate good will; the practice may have originated as a gesture demonstrating that a person's hand did not hold a weapon.

Missing out on the opportunity to shake hands when greeting someone not only makes the other person feel uncomfortable, it is a social slight. Have you ever been left out of a handshaking session among a group meeting at a reception or dinner? Then you know what I am talking about. Missing that opportunity leaves that person feeling left out the rest of the event. By the way, if you travel to other countries, brush up on their form of greeting. The rule is to use the host country's form of greeting when in their country. In the United States, you are never wrong to offer a handshake.

Handshaking Sensitivities:

What if someone doesn't raise their hand?
Or, what if they are in a wheelchair?

Be aware of someone's inability to shake hands. Some people may not want to or cannot shake your hand. Not to worry. If their hand does not come up, simply put your hand down and go on introducing yourself with a warm smile.

Sometimes a person may suffer from arthritis and not welcome a particularly strong handshake. Watch for signs of this before you grasp someone's hand. You can usually tell by looking at their eyes as well as their hand – it may be very slow in coming up for the shake, or they may wait a minute and hesitate. If they do so, don't reach over to grab their hand. Wait, they may explain the situation, or you can simply keep introducing yourself without the handshake.

If the person happens to be seated in a wheelchair, shake their hand just like you would anyone else, but step to your left of their chair to get closer to their hand. If they do not lift their hand for the shake, it is considered appropriate for you to go ahead and lightly touch the top of their hand (not pat!) while saying hello and introducing yourself, then step back. Please do not ever touch any other part of someone's body or lean on their wheelchair.

What about germs – yuck!

I realize germs are transmitted when shaking hands; unfortunately, this does not let you off the hook! Having said that, while I do realize that we cannot always stay home, it would be preferable to coughing and sneezing at a special event or reception. If it cannot be helped, excuse yourself from shaking hands by saying something like, "Please excuse me; I'm unable to shake your hand because of this nasty cold." Then go ahead with your introduction and conversation. Have your handkerchief ready in case you feel a sneeze coming on, and try your best to leave the room for a sneeze.

When do I actually start talking?

This has turned out to be quite confusing for people. My clients are always asking me, "Who speaks first?" Because I want people to feel comfortable stepping up to the plate, my answer is always the same – YOU! However, usually the person serving as a "host" at an event, or the person welcoming you into a room, is the person who extends a hand for shaking and also speaks first, but this isn't always the case. If you sense that the "host" person is not going to approach you, feel free to step in for the handshake and introduce yourself, "Hello, my name is Frank Finesse." It is much better than allowing the moment to become awkward. Feel free to look at the person's nametag, usually worn on the right-hand side of the chest for easy reading when handshaking.

What about teenagers – do I shake their hand as well?

Yes! Interestingly, this question comes up frequently – almost as often as comments about how teenagers "don't know how to shake hands." In fact, it's best to teach your children to shake hands as early as possible – before they are teenagers! Children should be taught to shake hands whenever they are meeting new people – neighbors, teachers, friends at church. Teach them to stand still, raise their hand from their elbow – holding it straight out – then grasp the person's hand firmly, and at the same time smile and look them in the eye. They should say, "Hello, my name is Tommy Brown." They should always respond using the adult's "honorific, e.g., Mr. or Ms." Such as – "It's nice to meet you, Mr. Smith." If you are considering whether it is appropriate to shake someone's hand, shake *everyone's* hand, then you don't have to worry!

What if someone gives me a terrible handshake?

Remember that "limp" handshake? Of course, you would never make a comment about someone else's handshake (even to another person). You can't manage someone else's shake, just give them your best one, and move on.

Does a woman stand for a handshake?

Yes. Business etiquette is the same for women and men, so women should stand for a handshake unless the other person tells them to stay seated. This may happen when people are already seated at a dinner table. It used to be that men were supposed to wait for a woman to raise a hand, but no more. Today, women should be assertive in extending a hand, as some men are still confused by this. This goes for both professional and personal situations.

Polishing your professional presence:

HANDSHAKING

1. Test your handshake with a good friend. It should be firm, but not too firm. A handshake is NOT a power play.

2. Shake hands when you first meet or see someone, and when you say good-bye.

3. Make good eye contact when shaking hands.

4. Handshaking is done standing up, if at all possible.

5. If you are seated behind a desk (with the exception of service positions such as bank tellers or hotel front desk staff), step around from your desk to shake hands. Preferably, there should be no barrier between you.

6. Your hand should come up from the elbow, and the hand should be straight (this helps avoid the "limp") handshake.

7. When you grasp the other person's hand, connect with the "web" of their hand (the area between the thumb and forefinger). This should help you shake the person's hand, not their fingers.

8. Shake two to three times, then let go. Do not "pump" the person's hand for an entire introduction!

9. Please do not touch the person's arm, shoulder, or pull them in for a hug (we'll talk about hugging later). And, unless you are a politician or a minister, do not clasp the person's hand with both of your hands while handshaking. This is considered very personal and is inappropriate, especially in business.

10. If you suffer from a sweaty palm, carry a handkerchief with you and step out of sight to periodically dry off your hand.

INTRODUCTIONS. DO IT.

Introductions are funny. Most people are not uncomfortable introducing *themselves*, but when it comes to bringing *others* together, their arm hairs stand on end and they freeze up! When I attended protocol school, we spent an entire day learning how to properly conduct introductions, which was much appreciated. I then agonized over a way to teach this art form in a *Reader's Digest* version, and here is what I came up with . . .

We tend to make it too complicated. The first rule of thumb is to DO IT. The biggest mistake made with regard to introductions is neglecting them, for conversation cannot take place without them. Have you ever sat down late at a banquet when everyone has already been introduced, only to be the one person at the table who doesn't know anyone and they don't know you? Awkward! So, before we go any further, just relax and understand that making the attempt to introduce people - even if it is done improperly – is much better than not trying at all.

Simple Business Introductions:

Business introductions are based on precedence (or order of importance) not gender. In other words, in a company, the highest ranking person's name is mentioned first. If you were introducing a CEO to a new Vice President, you would say:

"Mr. Greg Smith (the CEO), may I introduce
Ms. Donna Brown (the VP)."

As they are shaking hands, go on to say something about the second person to help the CEO out in welcoming her if you can. Say something like:

"Ms. Brown has just flown in from Miami
to join us for tonight's Annual Meeting."

Does this make sense? You could change your wording a bit and say, "may I present," or "I would like to introduce," but please do not say, "I would like you to meet." As the introducer, you are simply bringing the people together, *performing the service of introducing them.* The fact that YOU would like them to meet doesn't matter. Always use "Mr. and Ms." in business introductions. In this example, after being introduced, the CEO might ask Ms. Brown to call him "Greg," and she would in turn ask him to call her "Donna." If this exchange does not happen, she would continue to call him "Mr. Smith" and he should call her "Ms. Brown."

Simple Social Introductions

Socially, the first name spoken is usually the woman's with the exception of formal introductions such as the introductions of chiefs of state or royalty, in which case their names are spoken first. For example, you might say something like this:

"Ms. Cashman, may I introduce Mr. Jones."

Or, if it is a less formal event where everyone is on a first-name basis, say:

"Karen Cashman, may I introduce Jim Jones."

Make your introduction even more pleasant by adding a bit of information that will help start conversation. Something like:

> *"Jim and I have been members of this organization*
> *for years, and he has done a wonderful job of organizing*
> *this event again this year."*

Introduction Sensitivities:

> *What if I am introducing someone to a few people?*

This often happens at receptions and dinners. Easy! Just say:

> *"Excuse me . . . may I introduce George Lopez."*

And then announce the names of the others in the group. If you cannot remember all of the names, it is perfectly acceptable for you to ask them to introduce themselves, such as:

> *"Excuse me . . . this is George Lopez.*
> *Let's take a moment to introduce ourselves."*

Even if you know one or two of the names, this option would be less awkward than introducing those people, then asking everyone else to self-introduce. (Then they would KNOW which ones you don't remember!)

> *I just hate it when a large home party comes to a screeching*
> *halt when a new person or couple arrives.*

> *Is it necessary to stop the party for introductions?*

This is a common misunderstanding. When a group of people is involved (not just a few in a conversation as mentioned above), the host should welcome newcomers at the door, take their coats, show them to the refreshments, and also introduce them to at least one other person or couple to integrate them into the function. Actually, it is inappropriate to stop everything and go around the room with introductions. Guests bear the responsibility of introducing themselves beyond this point!

What if I cannot remember the person's name?

While I do encourage people to work hard to remember people's names, this is a common occurrence. First, feel free to look at the person's nametag, if there is one. (Nametags should be worn on the person's right-hand side for clear viewing; this is the same hand used for handshaking, so the eye can easily view the nametag.) If there is no nametag, make eye contact with a warm smile, and extend your hand for a handshake – then say YOUR name. "Hello, Stephanie Horton." This is your way of hinting to the other person that you would appreciate them giving THEIR name. If none of this works, don't feel embarrassed, just say something that fits your personality. I like to say, "Please help me remember your name." Then, do not go into a fit of apologies about forgetting, just move on with the conversation.

I'm not sure I can pronounce the name – what do I do?

It's so important to pronounce someone's name correctly, show style by asking for help. Say something like, "Would you mind telling me your name again? I would like to be able to pronounce it properly."

Polishing your professional presence:

INTRODUCTIONS

1. Make comfortable eye contact when introducing yourself; do not stare.

2. Always include everyone when making introductions, even if you must ask them to introduce themselves.

3. It is perfectly acceptable to view someone's nametag to capture their name.

4. Introductions should be made while standing up; try to stand from a dining table, but if the person approaching you says to remain seated, then do so.

5. Please don't make comments about a person's country of origin or ask them such questions.

6. Please don't make hand gestures or touch the people you are introducing.

7. Refrain from making inappropriate comments about the last time you saw the person, such as, "Last time I saw you, you were with . . ." Remember, if you embarrass that person, they will disappear from the radar in your world!

MEETING PEOPLE WITH DISABILITIES

There are more than 35 million people with disabilities in the United States. Some of them are your neighbors, relatives, and your friends at work. A person with a disability should be given the same respect you would extend to someone else.

The following guidelines from the national Easter Seal Society will help you focus on a person's ability, rather than his/her disability:

When introduced to a person with a disability, offer to shake hands. Persons with limited hand use or who wear an artificial limb can shake hands. However, some people do not have use of their hands. In this case, lean forward slightly – enough so that you can reach their hand – then put your hand on top of theirs just for a second, then greet them, then stand back. Do not pat their hand or touch their shoulder or any part of their body, or stand too close to their wheelchair.

When talking with a person who has a disability, speak directly to them rather than through a companion. If you offer to help, wait until the offer has been accepted, then listen or ask for instructions.

Don't be embarrassed if you happen to use words that seem to relate to a disability; i.e., "See you later, "Walk this way," etc. are common expressions that everyone uses. Don't use the word *handicap*. A disabling condition may or may not be handicapping; use *disability* rather than *handicap*. For example, persons who have paralysis and must use wheelchairs are handicapped by stairs. The term *physically challenged* may be used instead of disability.

Remember to shake hands again when you are ready to leave a conversation, and say, "It was nice talking with you. I hope we meet again."

And, please do not lean upon someone's wheelchair, or touch them other than while handshaking. The wheelchair is considered part of an individual's personal space.

— Chapter 4 —
Extra Touches
Hugging & Business Cards

HUGGING: AVOID IT!

Hugging has become such a part of American life that it deserves plenty of attention. Let me start by saying that I *am* a hugger. I hug my friends, but I do not hug business people I barely know. Where this becomes confusing is when business associates *become* friends. My advice is to know the difference and proceed with caution. Here's why: hugging is not about you. Remember what we said about making people comfortable?

You would not believe how many people wait to see me after my talks around the country to ask me, "Stephanie, how can I get people to stop hugging me?" It is not because they are mean or impersonal folks, and that really isn't the point. The point is that hugging and touching someone *is* personal, too personal. And it makes people very uncomfortable. Remember that it would be a breach of etiquette for someone to tell you to stop hugging them because it would make *you* uncomfortable.

To be clear, in our culture, people like to have 2-3 feet as a "comfort zone" around them when interacting with others. When you step inside this circle, you are entering their personal zone, and risk making them very uneasy.

If you are still having trouble with this, think about those who have had injuries or surgeries, those who have muscle disorders or weight issues, or maybe they simply don't like being squeezed by someone they do not consider a close and personal friend. It's kind of like having the checker at the grocery store call you by your first name when you do not know them at all. It crosses a line.

The bottom line on hugging: save it for your family and friends, and even then be careful.

BUSINESS CARD PROTOCOL

Some people have developed the habit of hardly looking at a business card when it is given to them without any thought of protocol or style. This is a big mistake, especially since it happens just at the moment you are getting to know someone for the first time. Your business card is as important as your handshake, your smile or your physical appearance when it comes to making a lasting impression and, as such, it should be handled in such a way that the recipient will be sure to remember you.

Whether you are here or abroad, remember these tips on business card etiquette:

Carry cards in a handsome leather or metal case to keep them fresh and protected. Never give out a card that is defective, out of date or soiled.

At a social function, exchange cards discreetly, away from the main event and host.

When visiting a client's company, always present your card to the receptionist.

Traveling internationally? Have cards printed with your name, title and company in English on one side and in the language of your host country on the other. Have it proofed by a colleague from the host country. In the host country, present your business card, native-language side up, with both hands.

When receiving a card, take it with both hands and study it carefully before putting it in your breast pocket or wallet. The greater the rank of the person presenting the card, the longer it should be studied. This is particularly appropriate in Japan, and has been adopted in the United States as well.

In a meeting, place the card on the table in front of you to help keep names, faces and positions straight. Do not write on the card in the presence of the person who gave it to you.

And, when you are attending banquets, do not pass around several of your business cards to your tablemates before you have met them – unless it is a networking event and you have been directed to do so. Giving and receiving business cards should be an extension of a personal business conversation.

— Part Three —
CONVERSATION ETIQUETTE

Conversation is an art form. It comes naturally for some people, but others really have to work at it. My clients often complain about having to attend parties and events, and when I ask them why, they say it is because they have difficulty making conversation. They find it difficult to think of topics and keep the conversation going. Sometimes I feel the same way! At one event, the conversation just flows and everyone has a great time, then the next party I attend things are a little more difficult. The point is, we all have to work at it. I'm hoping this section will help you feel more comfortable and prepare you for the next conversation at hand.

> *Good humor is a tonic for mind and body.*
> *It is the best antidote for anxiety and depression.*
> *It is a business asset. –Glenville Kleiser*

Here's what's driving people crazy –

1. People insist on telling me private details about their relationships.

2. People brag continuously about their newborns or children in a business setting.

3. Someone pats pregnant women on the stomach – or even worse, congratulates them or makes a comment about it when they aren't even pregnant!

4. People I barely know hug me in a business setting or continuously pat me on the back or touch me while talking with me.

5. Swear words are used, whether in a business or social setting, especially around young people.

—— *Chapter 5* ——
Business Conversation

This topic deserves its own section, especially in an etiquette book. Let me say that given all of the etiquette guidelines discussed in this book, I'm hoping that by helping you have a comfortable knowledge of *what* to do or *how* to do some things will leave your mind clear for what's truly important – the conversation at hand.

Whether business or pleasure, conversation should take the highest priority. While it's true that someone may be as put off by a bad handshake as bad conversation, the two really do go hand in hand (pardon the pun)!

In the United States, business is commonly conducted over meals. Make this objective known when extending the meal invitation so that everyone will know what to expect. If the objective is social only – to have fun and get to know each other – convey that intent as well.

At a business meal, spend the first ten minutes getting to know each other and establishing rapport then proceed to the business conversation. Some people wait until the main course is served for this purpose.

Let's move on. You are hosting an important business meal. Your table manners are impeccable, you are dressed to kill, and you are having a great time with your clients. Then you begin talking about your recent operation and how nauseated you became afterwards. Or, you are on a diet and comment on the fat content of everything at the table. Or, you are going through a nasty breakup and feel the need to share the latest drama. All - inappropriate table talk!

When deciding what to talk about, think about how someone could respond to a statement you make. For example, if you say, "I just had my gallbladder removed," what would someone's response be? If you say, "I'm going through a divorce right now," what kind of response is in order? Obviously, the person would say they are sorry, putting your conversation in a downward spin from the get-go.

As I mentioned, I consider small talk to be an art form, but it is never "small" in importance. When talking about "table talk," I encourage all things positive. It's an easy way to remember what might be appropriate.

For example, make a comment about how interesting the speaker is, how beautiful the building is, or the city in which you are dining. Start with your surroundings. All comments should be positive. Don't run the risk of insulting someone by making a negative comment about the building; the person sitting next to you might own it.

Prepare for business meals by reading newspapers, trade magazines and especially any specific information about your client's company. For example, they may be building a new corporate headquarters or have recently launched a new product. Wouldn't it be better to cement your relationships by bringing up these topics rather than commenting on the weather?

Don't ask too many questions, and, most importantly, LISTEN to your client's responses. You can tell if you are treading on thin ice; change the topic. Often the answers will help you come up with additional topics. Listen carefully. This is the most important advice I can convey. If you listen and genuinely care about what someone is saying, the conversation will take care of itself; i.e., you can build your topics and questions from what others are already saying.

GETTING PERSONAL

Be careful. Especially in business, personal questions are not appreciated. Please do not ask questions about a person's lifestyle, such as whether they are married, whether they have children, etc. It is okay to ask them where they are from or where they live, but please do not ask them why they don't have children, why they are divorced, or how long they have been married – all considered too personal. However, if someone brings up their family life, such as that their children play sports, feel free to follow-up on that specific topic.

If they insist on bringing up inappropriate topics, do your best to change the subject.

THE ULTIMATE BORE

This person talks about himself. You know who I'm talking about. Every time you share a story about something you have done, he has done it, done it more times, and done it better than you. To be a brilliant conversationalist, comment on what someone else had said, and ask for more information – do NOT give your own experience. Wait to be asked, or wait for the appropriate time. You might test the waters by saying something like, "I know what you mean; I've had a similar experience." If they don't ask, move on to something else. Do not say, "Here's what happened to ME . . . ."

LANGUAGE, LANGUAGE, LANGUAGE

As in other matters of etiquette, first and foremost is the comfort of the people around you, and this includes the use of any type of foul or inappropriate language. I know YOU wouldn't even think of swearing, for example, but there are some words that are creeping into our popular culture that may not be considered swearing, but should also be avoided at all costs.

Let's just say it – saying "that sucks," "I was so pissed off," or using the word "crap" are all inappropriate, and, unfortunately, are all used on network television these days. Another one that people find annoying (especially internationals) is the American way of referring to everyone as "you guys." If you travel abroad, you may have already been called on this one. I have had several clients tell me that this really lowers the bar in professional circles; it is simply language that is casual to a fault, and somewhat dismissive. It is not necessary to address a group of people at all. No need to say "you all" or "you guys." Simply say, "hello" or "good evening." Again, no one will tell you, they will just let it steam and simmer.

Here's where I run the risk of having you think I am totally NO FUN, but I assure you that's not true! The easiest way to clear this language from your vocabulary is to remove it altogether. Never use it. Otherwise, it is easy for it to slip out at the most inconvenient times. And using it at home is how it spreads to our children.

TAKING NOTES AT THE TABLE

Usually this would occur at a business luncheon; rarely would you be conducting business that would require note taking at a dinner. If the topic warrants it, ask if your client minds if you take notes; keep a *small* pad (not a giant yellow legal pad) on hand for this purpose. Usually your client will be complimented by your serious interest in following up. Remember to maintain good eye contact, and be aware of the wait staff — nothing more embarrassing than leaving a pen mark on a server's sleeve.

TABLE-HOPPING

While sociability is a desirable trait, table-hopping is totally inappropriate. Keep your conversation to your own table. It's okay to acknowledge others with a smile and nod, but do not stop to chat. You will be interrupting their conversation as well as your own.

Polishing your professional presence:

THE SPOKEN WORD

1. Good conversationalists understand that listening is more important than talking, and look for opportunities to ask follow-up questions.

2. When attending receptions or events, it is acceptable to hold a five-minute conversation, then move on by saying something like, "It has been so nice talking with you. I hope you enjoy the convention." Then you may exit.

3. For a professional presence, always stand and sit tall, with your back straight and hands to your sides. Do not sway or put your hands in your pockets.

4. Never ask personal questions, such as whether a person is married, has children, or – why not?

5. Do not make assumptions about people and their relationships, or ask them questions like, "Is that your boyfriend?" or assume that a woman on a man's arm is his wife. Listen to how the person is introduced, and follow that lead. The woman may, in fact, be his spouse but may use her maiden name.

— *Part Four* —
MEETING MANNERS

Even though we are living in the age of technology, meeting with people face-to-face is still a mainstay of today's business communications. If you cringe at the idea of presenting your ideas in front of a group, introducing yourself to the big boss or facilitating a meeting, this is a good time to brush up on your basic meeting skills. Listening plays a huge role in appropriate meeting behavior, as does scheduling the right time, the appropriate people, and the all-important follow-up tasks.

Half of the world is on the wrong scent in the pursuit of happiness. They think it consists in having and getting, and in being served by others. It consists of giving and serving others. –Henry Drummond

Here's what's driving people crazy –

1. People crash into my office for impromptu meetings without an appointment.

2. People answer the phone while I am having a meeting with them to carry on a personal conversation with their sister from Topeka.

3. People use cell phones in a restroom stall!

4. Certain associates are never prepared for meetings.

5. My boss embarrasses me at a meeting by – *surprise* – asking for information I am not prepared to provide.

6. I am invited to a dinner meeting, and my host arrives late.

7. People carry on "side" conversations during meetings and meals.

8. People answer cell phones during meetings.

— Chapter 6 —
Impromptu and Scheduled Meetings

IMPROMPTU MEETINGS

Warning! Starting up an unexpected meeting may *not* be the way to go! If your company occupies an open office landscape, you are probably aware of this problem – painfully. Impromptu meetings occur when people: "pop" into your office unannounced; stretch over the top of the cubicle wall to ask you a question; stand behind you while you are working on the computer, just waiting for you to pause and look up; follow you down the hall asking you questions; or — my favorite – they follow you into the restroom.

If you would like to win or remain in someone's favor, it is best to clarify in advance how they would like to communicate. In my former career, I had one boss who wanted us to leave important notes and messages on his chair. When he left the company, his replacement came to my office asking me why I kept leaving notes on her chair! Instead of assuming that is the way she preferred to do business, I should have asked. Clarity is important. Sometimes management will say they have an "open door policy" – what does this mean, exactly? Some upper management appreciates it when their employees stop by with an overview of the day's activities; some do NOT. There is value in clarity.

By the way, the same communication needs ring true for your workmates. At a group meeting, it is worthwhile to discuss how it is best to handle communications procedures, in general. Take the time to discuss it as a group – then stick by what the group decides.

If someone pops in unannounced, welcome them with a smile, and if you are unable to talk with them at that moment, ask them if they would like to set up a special time to chat later in the day, as you are working on a deadline or special project. Or, encourage them to email you with their questions so that you have time to prepare. If you hold long – especially personal – conversations with people at your desk, what does it say to others? You *must* like it!

SCHEDULED BUSINESS MEETINGS

Planning is the key for scheduled business meetings. Do you frequently serve as the chair? If so, minding your meeting manners will serve you and your staff well. There is more to knowing your *role* at the meeting than knowing which *roll* is yours!

Consider yourself the "producer" of the meeting – think through everything from the meeting agenda to the invitation list. Are all of the appropriate people and decision makers included? Is the meeting scheduled at the most convenient time possible for everyone involved? Mornings tend to be best, especially for the more challenging topics.

The style of seating can help your meeting atmosphere. To encourage team conversation, use round tables with seating around half of the table. For pure lectures, consider classroom-style seating. Remember that theatre-style seating with no tables is not comfortable for note-taking.

Communication is vital. Attendees appreciate knowing all about the meeting, and especially appreciate getting an advance copy of the agenda. What are your expectations of them? The clearer you communicate those expectations, the better.

Nothing is too small for your attention. The more importance you give meeting details upfront, the more those involved will appreciate your effort and, in response, will be more likely to actively participate. Once the stage is set, your role is to make everyone feel comfortable and appreciated, keep the agenda on-track, and the room the correct temperature.

Want to deter latecomers? Begin *every* meeting ON TIME by going around the room and shaking hands with everyone personally. As latecomers arrive, stop everything to go over and welcome them the same way. This approach works!

When teaching at a local community college, I quickly recognized that tardiness was a problem that made it difficult to accomplish our class goals in the two days per week our class met. I announced to the class that in order for us to "do business" in class together like in the real business world, I would greet every class member with a handshake. And, I told them that the latecomers could simply come to the front of the class when they arrived so that I could greet them politely in the same manner. You guessed it – from that day forward, they were there ten minutes early! A side benefit of this exercise was that I learned the students' names, helping me get to know them and connect with them throughout the quarter.

—— Chapter 7 ——
Meeting over Cocktails and Meals

BREAKFAST AND LUNCHEON MEETINGS

Dining details aside, let's focus for a moment on the concept of meeting over meals. Unlike some other countries, in the United States, it is common practice for business to be conducted at mealtime. I suggest you research your clients carefully. Doing business over meals may make them uncomfortable – thus impossible for you to meet your business objectives. Internationally, business meetings usually take place in an office, with mealtime reserved for getting to know you better and entertainment.   Having said that, business breakfasts and lunches are the most common, followed by dinner.

Breakfast and lunch meetings work well for very busy people. Discuss your guest's schedule carefully, and be on time! Make sure to set an end time to your meeting and stick to it. If at all possible, offer to pick up your guest. While they may not take you up on your offer, it will be appreciated.

Tell your guest exactly where you will meet them. When dining in hotels or restaurants, it is best to meet in the foyer of the restaurant area. You should wait there for them; do not sit at your table. If you must be seated (there is no waiting area), sit at the table, but do not touch anything, not even your napkin. Keep everything beautiful for your guest's arrival.

Call your guest the day before to confirm all of the arrangements. Make no assumptions! I cannot believe the number of times people have related meeting nightmare stories about waiting for clients in the wrong restaurant or hotel. Sometimes chain restaurants and hotels confuse the issue. I'm sure it goes without saying, but here goes – *make reservations!*

COCKTAIL AND DINNER MEETINGS

These work best for mixing business and pleasure, turning a meeting more into entertainment. If you are entertaining a client who is traveling to your city, it is often much appreciated to be invited to dinner. However, this becomes a less attractive option for those who live in the area. People are very sensitive about giving up treasured family time for business meetings – not always, but frequently. For this reason, consider inviting them to bring a guest as well. And remember, table conversation should include everyone.

Cocktail meetings are less popular these days, but drinks may be served with your dinner meeting. I would encourage inviting your guests for both cocktails and dinner, and avoid a "cocktail only" invite. We'll cover how to manage alcohol, etc., in a later chapter. (See page 62.)

Polishing your professional presence:

AT MEETINGS

1. Welcome everyone with a warm handshake and smile.

2. Listen with undivided attention.

3. Introduce everyone, and acknowledge latecomers.

4. Speak at a comfortable and pleasing pace.

5. Don't interrupt.

6. Stay focused, and follow the agenda.

7. If topics get off-course, suggest an "offline" discussion or later meeting. List the subject matter on a flip chart (frequently referred to as a "parking lot") so that the topic can be brought up next meeting or handled in some other way.

8. Call people by name.

9. Enthusiastically acknowledge and write down any ideas, suggestions or comments. Remember, every idea is a gift, and if we stop encouraging them, they will stop coming.

10. Thank everyone for their "enthusiastic" participation. Let them know that you appreciate it!

— *Part Five* —
THE ART OF DINING

Are you nervous about dining with clients – or maybe a date? If so, you are not alone. If you think about it, dining is really a matter of common sense. The idea is to make the dining experience enjoyable and beautiful for everyone involved, including YOU! From your clothing to your conversation and attitude, approach everything with a positive attitude and you will be off to the right start. Just remember, dining is really not about food, it is about people. The food is secondary. Spending time with special people is what is truly important.

> *It isn't so much what's on the table that matters,*
> *as what's on the chairs. –W.S. Gilbert*

Here's what's driving people crazy –

1. People tell inappropriate jokes at the dinner table.

2. People make fun of others' dining mishaps, such as spilled drinks.

3. People complain about the quality of the food or drinks.

4. I feel pressured to order another cocktail or glass of wine.

5. People stack a bread and butter plate on top of the salad plate when finished.

6. People turn their glasses and coffee cups upside down.

7. My tablemates are up and down talking to the people at the next table.

8. Someone spits food into their napkin! (Napkins are not to be used as receptacles.)

9. My dining partner uses a napkin as a handkerchief.

10. People place a used napkin over the top of their plate when finished.

11. People pile used dishes onto the next table.

12. My tablemates shake hands in front of my face – elbow!

13. Someone snaps their fingers to get the attention of the wait staff.

— Chapter 8 —
The Big Picture
Are you the Host or Guest?

First, think about the big picture – decide upon your "dining objective." Just like any other gathering, there should be a clear objective; i.e., why are you attending or hosting this meal? This should help when considering everything from the room and the mood to the food. For example, if you are hosting a meal to honor someone for a promotion, and other non-business guests are involved, chose a very nice restaurant that would appeal to everyone, a place where your guests will feel special and pampered. This is not the time to go where you would have to talk over videos and bar trivia games.

On the other hand, if you are meeting someone for a blind date, perhaps an informal restaurant full of lively people and conversation would be a good choice, to help relieve the initial stress of the first meeting.

Are you the HOST or the GUEST? It makes a huge difference. Your role as a host is completely different than that of a guest. The person who does the inviting is the host and is "in charge" of the evening. This is the person who pays the check. If you are the guest, you are essentially receiving the gift of the meal or evening, and should follow the host's lead when it comes to ordering, etc. Remember, you are receiving a gift. Let's take a look at host and guest duties, the first step in the art of dining . . .

*If you are the HOST, y*ou are responsible for this meal function — Its success or failure is up to you. All decisions should be made with your guest's good time and comfort in mind. If it is the first time you are having a meal with this guest, choose an All-American-type restaurant with many menu choices, then start a conversation about good food during your meal to learn their favorites. Make a note of it! And next time invite them to one of their other favorite restaurants.

Since you – as the host — have chosen the restaurant or facility, it better be good! (It is up to the host to choose the restaurant.) If you are out of town, call upon the local Convention & Visitors Bureau or State Restaurant Association for assistance in choosing a restaurant. If you are staying in a hotel, use the concierge service. They will also make reservations for you, and often will be able to secure the best tables in town.

If possible, dine at the restaurant in advance. This provides several advantages. You will be able to personally observe the staff, see what the table options are, and generally become comfortable with the facility. I recommend you use the same restaurant as much as possible; you will be treated like royalty.

Here's a few tips for the big night:

1. Arrive early to introduce yourself to the actual staff that will be serving you (they'll appreciate knowing who the host is). The level of service you receive may depend upon the respect you give the staff. Treat ALL MEMBERS of a restaurant staff with dignity and grace, and you should receive the same in return.

2. If possible, arrange for the bill to be handled after your guests leave, or away from the table. Ask the staff how best to handle this. This is a great way for women to pick up the check without any kind of conflict, which still can happen even in today's enlightened times (whoever invites pays).

3. Check the table presentation, table settings, and discuss the menu options.

4. Check the restrooms to make sure they are clean and accessible for your guests (yes!!!).

5. Meet your guests in the lobby, or near the entrance to the dining room.

6. Please note the difference between a large function and a small dinner party. At a large function, it is your job to greet people at the door, and perhaps introduce them to one other couple or person. It is not your job to introduce them to everyone at the function. At a small dinner party, you should introduce all of the guests to one another.

7. If you must be seated (sometimes there is not a waiting area), do not touch anything on the table. Seat yourself so that you can see when your guest arrives.

8. Follow the restaurant hostess to the table, and assure that your guest gets the best seat. Generally, the best seat in the house is the one with the view of the room and/or the view of the water or city – not the view of the server station or wall. Do not allow yourself to be seated near a restroom door. (Again – getting there early helps.)

A few words about ordering: Your guests should order first. As host, your job is to offer your guest the world by suggesting fine and expensive menu items, so your guest will feel comfortable ordering them. Feel free to offer recommendations, but do not push. If your guest orders an expensive item, order one in a similar price range. Also, you should order the same courses as your guest. For example, if your guest orders an appetizer, so should you. This way, you will both be dining at the same pace. It is very awkward when one person is eating a salad and the other is sitting there staring!

What about wine? Tell your guest you are thinking of ordering a bottle of wine with dinner, to see if they are interested. If so, ask what type of wine they enjoy, then order the best you can. If you do not drink, and only two of you are dining, it is appropriate to suggest wine by the glass.

You should watch to see if your guest is enjoying his/her wine and food. You might notice that they haven't touch their food or drink. If not, ask <u>once</u>

if they would like something else. Do not ask again or embarrass them by asking what is wrong with it. They simply may not be hungry, or may be saving up for a later course.

Here's a few more tips for a memorable dining experience at the table:

1. Dine at a reasonable speed — not too fast or slow. Try to match the pace of your guests, but remember — they are watching you to pace themselves!

2. If something falls on the floor, leave it there unless it presents a danger to others (tell the server).

3. If food falls off the plate, leave it there. The server will dispose of it.

4. If there are not enough utensils, use what is there — the server will bring more. Never yell for a server, simply sit up and look around the room. They will come.

5. You should keep everyone engaged in appropriate dinner conversation.

If you are the GUEST, you are not in charge, but you still have a role! In general, you should be appreciative, complimentary, and supportive of your host's offerings. You are receiving this gift of a meal, and should remain positive at all costs. You should not criticize the restaurant, prior service, or mention anything negative. Keep the conversation positive. It never fails, the first time we complain about the food or service, it turns out the host's father-in-law owns the place.

Generally, you should follow your host's lead; do not even remove your napkin until your host does. **Here are a few tips for the guest:**

1. Try not to communicate directly with the server; your host will be watching you, and meeting your needs. For example, do not ask for more bread or water. Just wait for the service to come to you.

2. Follow your host's lead to order — see what he/she suggests. Order the same courses they order, so that you will eat together throughout the meal.

3. If you do not drink, do not be compelled to order wine. Simply say, "A mineral water with lime would be wonderful, thank you." Never feel compelled to explain why you are NOT ordering an alcoholic beverage. In most situations, it is prudent to order a non-alcoholic drink first, then see how the evening progresses and discover whether the host is ordering wine.

4. If you do not like something on your plate, try to take a few bites, but do not comment.

5. If your food is not prepared properly, try to deal with it, unless it will make you sick. If so, wait for the server to come to your aid, and QUIETLY ask for another plate. Don't get into a big conversation about the food or argue, at any cost. Your host should notice that you are not eating, and ask you if you would like something else. If so, feel free to take them up on the offer. Don't go into big explanations ("I just can't eat this, etc."), just order another selection or whatever.

6. Dine at the same speed as your host. It is no fun to host a meal and watch the food be devoured seemingly without being tasted!

7. Do not offer to buy wine or pay for anything else, such as the tip. This is your host's party. Do not interrupt it. It is not appropriate to reciprocate for a "gift" during the gift. Perhaps you can invite the person for a meal next time. However -

8. If you are traveling together, or have decided to go somewhere else for an after dinner drink, it is appropriate for you to invite/suggest/pay for that.

9. At a small party, wait for the host to introduce you to the other guests; at a large party, feel free to introduce yourself.

── Chapter 9 ──
Dining Details

Now that you have the host vs. guest roles in mind, let's tackle the topic of dining in more detail. Dining is all about keeping the table – and yourself – viewed as beautifully as possible. Here's where "beautiful" manners really come into play. From your personal presence to how you cut your meat, think about creating a beautiful experience for those around you, whether you are the host or guest.

Why is this so important? It puts people at ease and ensures a great experience. If your overuse of perfume or cologne is making your dining mates sick or you stuff an entire roll in your mouth at one time, this sets the stage for a dining disaster, business or personal! Let's get started.

NAPKIN, PLEASE!

Once the host is seated, he/she will place their napkin on their lap. A dinner napkin should be folded in half, with the fold to your waist. When using the napkin, select a corner, and pat your mouth; do not wipe your face. If you have to leave the table, please simply say "excuse me," to those around you (not necessary to call the media), and leave. We don't need to know where you are going.

My pet peeve, and sorry to be so detailed, but I must mention that "I have to go pee" is not acceptable language, and the sooner we start discouraging this with children, the better, in my opinion! And, when you leave the table, your napkin should be placed on your chair, not on the table. Why? Because you wouldn't want your germ-filled napkin to touch the clean table linen, right? A soiled napkin should not be placed on the table until the meal has ended, and everyone is leaving the table. During a luncheon where there is a speaker, for example, sit with your napkin on your lap throughout until everyone leaves the table.

Please do not tuck a napkin into your shirt collar unless you are attending a backyard barbeque and bibs are not provided! Don't spit anything such as a bone, rock, or other alien object into a napkin. It is not a receptacle. These items should be picked out with your fingers or spit back onto your fork, then placed back onto the plate.

Should your napkin fall to the floor, leave it there, and discreetly ask the server for another one.

ORDERING FOOD AND BEVERAGES

Follow the lead of the host in ordering, and perhaps take their suggestions if you like; make quick friends by NEVER ordering the most expensive item on a menu (the host will suggest such items as a courtesy), business or pleasure. In dining for business or pleasure, I generally recommend not partaking in a buffet, because it disturbs your flow of conversation and inhibits your ability to get to know each other. One exception to this is if someone invites you especially for a seafood buffet or barbeque. Keep in mind – order the same courses as your host or guest – if they order the buffet, go for it!

ABOUT ALCOHOL

The three-martini lunch is a thing of the past (heavy sigh). It is inappropriate to ask people if they drink – or why they don't – as it is for you to mention that YOU don't drink. Simply order a nonalcoholic beverage and let it go at that.

The story about why someone doesn't drink is too personal to share, and is no one's business.

When you are the host, offer your guests the world, such as "Would you like something to drink?" in a general way. As the guest, respond with a nonalcoholic choice at a business event, something such as iced tea or mineral water. I recommend noncarbonated beverages for obvious reasons! If your host mentions that they were thinking of ordering a bottle of wine with dinner, then either tell them that would be wonderful, or mention that you are very happy with your iced tea. It should be over at that.

If you do drink, play it smart. Limit yourself to one cocktail and preferably one glass of wine at dinner. Don't ever comment on someone else's consumption of wine, unless there is a problem and you have to call them a cab. For example, don't say "I wish I could drink as much as you, but . . ." or "If I drink more than one glass I will never make it in the morning." Resist the urge to comment.

If you do not want the server to refill your wine glass, place your fingers lightly over the glass before they pour. Sometimes they will take the glass away when you are through. Do not turn your wine glass upside down (or ever turn any of your other glassware, including coffee cups, upside down). One should not move any items – from silverware to glassware and plates – they should remain where the server places them.

I'm sure I don't need to mention overindulging, either at a business event or personally speaking. There are too many reasons to get into, and I'm sure you are aware. If you are on a job interview, don't drink. Period. If you are on a first date, drinking shots might not be impressive to a new person in your life. Think it through first.

UNDERSTANDING THE TABLE SETTING

Table settings can be intimidating, but there's a simple remedy: use the silverware from the outside in, including glassware. Note that your water glass will usually be placed above the knife. With a little practice, you will know what you are about to be served by the way the silverware has been set; the more courses, the more knives and forks. But be aware – sometimes silverware is served individually by the wait staff. Don't be thrown off by this, simply take the chilled fork or whatever as it is presented to you.

Also notice in the drawing that the solid items, such as a bread and butter plate, are placed to the left of the plate, and the glasses are placed to the right. Now you will never eat someone else's roll again!

Informal Setting *(See appendix for formal setting.)*

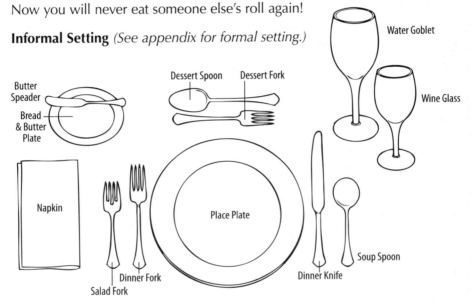

Water Goblet

Dessert Spoon   Dessert Fork

Butter
Speader

Bread
& Butter
Plate

Wine Glass

Napkin

Place Plate

Soup Spoon

Dinner Knife

Dinner Fork

Salad Fork

Handling the Knife and Fork

In the United States, most of use the "American" style of dining. This means we use the right hand to hold the knife while cutting food, then transfer the fork to the right hand to bring the food to our mouth.

The "Continental" or "International" style is considered more formal, but is also correct. If you are comfortable with it, it is the preferred choice, as it is generally the style of dining internationally. In the Continental style, the fork stays in the left hand and the knife (in the right hand) pushes the food onto the fork. The fork is brought to the mouth with the left hand, and tines of the fork in the down position.

Use whatever style is most comfortable for you. Just because someone else is dining with the Continental style, you don't have to, just be consistent throughout the meal.

To master the skill, next time you dine, take a look at how you hold your silverware. Do you look like you are going to attack something? Check out these illustrations to make sure you are on the right track toward beautiful dining:

The "Resting" Position

When you are not using your silverware (taking a little break for conversation or perhaps leaving the table), do not lean the silverware half onto the plate and half onto the table, like oars in a boat. Put them carefully on the plate. In the **American** style, place your knife (with blade down) and fork diagonally across your plate with a large space between them, as shown on the right).

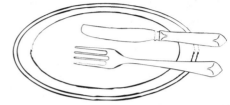

In the **Continental** style, cross your fork and knife (as shown). Wait staff will not remove your plate if your utensils are positioned like this.

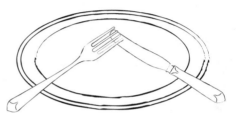

The "I am Finished" Position

When you are finished with a course, place the knife and fork across your plate as shown, tines of the fork either up or down. This is correct for both **American** and **Continental** styles.

Silverware Tips

Now that you know how to hold and place silverware when you are not eating, here's a few tips for silverware use:

1. Do not point or use your silverware to "draw" on the table or point while talking.

2. When cutting meat, pull the knife toward yourself; do not "saw" to prevent slippage.

3. Do not put too much food on your fork.

4. Take very small bites for a number of reasons; primarily, to prevent you from choking. Also, if you have a "problem" such as a piece of bone or rock in your food, it is easier to deal with if it is small. Either spit it carefully back onto the fork and quietly place it back onto your plate, or take it out of your mouth with your fingers and put it onto the plate – the plate from where it came. Please don't put it on your coffee cup saucer or bread and butter plate. Again, think *beauty*. If you put it back on the entré plate, it will be removed faster and won't be sitting around for everyone to see. And, resist the temptation to discuss it!! "What *is* this thing?"

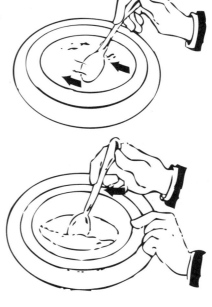

Eating Soup

To eat soup, spoon away from yourself and sip the spoon from the side, not from the front (you will not place the entire spoon in your mouth usually).

If you are served with a soup plate (shown), it is acceptable to tip the soup plate away from you to retrieve the last few drops. When you are finished, leave the spoon in the soup plate. If the soup is served in a soup cup, leave the spoon on the saucer rather in the cup where it could easily tip out. Refer to the Appendix for tips on eating specific foods.

Dessert

A good host should always offer (but not *push*) their guests a wonderful dessert. You might be surprised at how many people LOVE dessert, and will plan their entire meal around what they are going to have. If you are hosting a business or social meal, and your guest says they don't "have room" for dessert, suggest an after-dinner drink (if appropriate) or coffee, then don't order dessert yourself. Remember, you are having the same courses as them. Likewise, if your guest does order dessert, order it yourself. If they offer to share, resist by saying something like, "Thank you, but please go ahead. I was thinking about ordering the . . ." This way, they can have the dessert they want without worrying about you. Many a meal has been blown at this point. How? By saying things like, "If I ate a dessert like that I would be as big as a house. How do you do it?" or "It must be nice to be able to eat like that!" EEEEEK!!!

—— Chapter 10 ——
At the Table – Things to Keep in Mind

SEATING

For a small group dining in a restaurant, you know that the client or special date gets the seat facing the room and/or the view. You should sit close enough to your guest to assure ease in conversation.

In business, if spouses or partners attend, seat them across from you. This will help assure that they will be included in your conversation. Nothing will spoil a business relationship faster than a client's spouse who felt excluded. By the way, this also applies to social gatherings. Be very, very careful to include everyone in conversation.

At an informal dinner party without high executives or dignitaries, the sexes are seated alternatively, with husbands and wives separated, often at different tables. This may seem awkward at first, but after you get used to it, you will notice how it provides for lively conversation with guests other than your partner. They've heard all your stories anyway!

At a formal meal, seating should be according to precedence and title. The host sits at the head of the table, with the co-host (sometimes spouse) seated at the other head of the table. The honored guest sits to the right of the host and the honored guest's spouse sits to the right of the co-host. For more details on this, I recommend Letitia Baldrige's *New Manners for New Times* *[a complete guide to etiquette]; 2003, Simon & Schuster.*

When it is time to dine, the host(ess) will invite you to be seated. Never approach the table until invited to do so. A man should help the woman to his right into her chair. He should also assist the woman to his left if there is no one to help her. This is a bit of a gray area in today's business world, but I believe it is still a nice touch when groups with spouses are going for dinner. If it is clearly a social function, this is expected.

The appropriate way to assist with seating is to stand behind the chair and pull it back. The woman will slide in from her left, sitting partially on the chair, leaning forward. The man then gently slides the chair in under her. He should not push it in too far; she will adjust it as necessary at this point. Repeat when the meal is over.

Ladies, if there is no one to assist you, seat yourself from your left. Once seated, good posture is key – rest your back against the back of the chair and keep both feet flat on the floor, as mentioned.

PURSE PLACEMENT

No matter what size, never place your purse on the dining table; slide it alongside you on your chair, or underneath, carefully placed so the servers will not trip over it!

SNEEZING AND NOSE BLOWING

Please do not sneeze into your napkin. If you feel an emergency sneeze coming on, pick up your napkin, hold it over your nose (to keep germs from getting out), sneeze delicately, then leave the table to blow your nose in the restroom. I must get detailed about this due to the number of questions I always get about sneezing and blowing the nose at the table. DON'T!!! Carry a linen handkerchief for emergencies, but GET AWAY FROM THE TABLE AS SOON AS POSSIBLE!! RUN AWAY! RUN AWAY!

WHERE TO PUT YOUR HANDS

In the American style of dining, rest both hands in your lap. In the International/Continental style, it is acceptable to rest the wrists on the table. You may also place one hand in the lap and rest your other wrist on the table, for either style.

HOW TO HOLD GLASSES

Tumbler-style glasses are held near the bottom of the glass. Small-stem glasses are held by the stem and large-bowled glasses are held with your hand surrounding the bowl, to prevent them from tipping over. It is okay to look gently into a glass when drinking to prevent spillage.

THANKING THE SERVERS

I am often asked about how to thank the wait staff. It is considered inappropriate to thank them throughout a meal for every service they provide. Not only does this interrupt the table's conversation, it causes stress for the servers. Imagine if they were forced to say "thank you" to banquet of 500 for every little thing? The meal would never be served. I recommend you look at the server when the water is poured – look up and give them a warm smile and "thank you" so that they know you are a nice person who appreciates their good service. Then, at the end of the meal thank them for their excellent service. They will appreciate it! (They will also appreciate your NOT chatting with them throughout a meal.) This doesn't mean there might not be a good-natured banter at an informal meal, especially a social meal, but keep it BRIEF! If you are on a date, this can be a deal breaker. Extensive conversation with a server is simply rude to your dining partner.

Polishing your presence

AT THE TABLE

1. Please don't rush through a meal; pace yourself to your dining partners.

2. Dine carefully and deliberately, and be mindful about your elbows. Are they in the way of your neighbor or server? Be aware at all times of how you are sitting in general – straight, with both feet on the floor, not wrapped around a chair leg.

3. Refrain from pointing, waving or clanging your silverware.

4. Please be careful about speaking too loudly or making unsavory noises.

5. Please don't talk with your mouth full or do anything that would make the meal unpleasant.

6. Don't mix your food together on the plate, or move or stack plates when you are finished.

7. Refrain from placing soiled silverware or napkins on the table (it places germs near your dining partners).

8. Do not apply lipstick at the table.

9. Take very small bites of food for ease of swallowing, appearance, and conversation.

10. Put your purse in or under your chair.

11. Use toothpicks in private, not at the table.

12. Take small sips of any type of drink, and only when your mouth is clear of food.

13. Sit with all four legs of your chair in place.

14. Please eat your own roll; it's on the left!

15. Carry a linen handkerchief, and use it only in case of emergencies (tissues tend to disintegrate).

16. Keep your elbows low and close to your body.

17. Shake hands before you are seated at a table; it is awkward and rude to reach across people to shake hands at the table.

—Part Six—

ATTENDING CONVENTIONS
AND SPECIAL EVENTS

Representing your company – and yourself – at conventions and special events is a regular part of corporate life, but one which has probably not been mentioned in college or professional training. However, these events are extremely important as they provide the stage for you to meet your peers, customers and special guests. Probably the most important thing to remember is that while these events can be fun, they are still business related and require your utmost in professional behavior at all times. This is not the time to have that third glass of wine, even though it is tempting! Whether you are the host or guest, just remember the business purpose at hand, and you will be guaranteed a great experience for all.

> *Luck is a matter of preparation meeting opportunity. –Oprah Winfrey*

Here's what's driving people crazy —

1. Attendees at events wear their nametags too low!

2. Convention exhibitors are too pushy when I visit their booths.

3. Attendees at dinner events don't bother to introduce themselves before joining the table for a meal.

4. People from the same company hang out together throughout a cocktail party or dinner and talk shop.

5. People try to balance food, drinks and handshaking at cocktail parties, or even ask someone else to hold their plate or drink.

6. Attendees don't warmly invite others to join in their conversation.

7. Someone sends an alternate to a special dinner when a specific invitation has been offered (invitations are meant only for those to whom they are addressed, unless otherwise indicated).

8. I am not informed in advance of special dress requirements, such as casual wear for an outdoor barbeque and campfire.

9. I hear about a special dinner that others have been invited to, but not me!

10. A special meal or entertainment is offered on the night of arrival after a big travel day.

—— Chapter 11 ——
What is your objective?

Making a great impression at gatherings actually begins before you leave your house or hotel room, and, in some cases, before you leave the office. Consider the time you are about to spend at any event – it could be an evening or a few days at a conference. It is worth planning ahead to maximize the experience, professionally and personally.

Think about every event, even if it is just a business lunch, as you would a business meeting. What is your objective for being there? Why are you attending? Who will be there that you should or would like to meet? Just like you would not walk into a business meeting without an agenda, what is your reason for attending events and receptions? There may be multiple objectives. You may be representing your company at a trade show, for example, during the day, "selling" or showcasing your product or service. Or, you may be representing your company by *attending* a trade show. What's the difference? Here's where some folks make a critical mistake in judgment. Just because you are not "officially" on duty at a convention does not mean you are "off duty." You are still representing your company, even if you are visiting trade show booths.

I always encourage my clients to think through exactly what their specific objectives are for attending any type of event. Just taking this first step of preparation can set the stage for success!

There are many opportunities to meet people at conventions and events – from the opening reception to the final banquet. It might even be appropriate for you to invite a client whom you know is attending to join you for the opening gala, for example. Or, perhaps you could arrange to meet them there. Think it through.

Most conventions or events have an "opening" cocktail reception – it is considered a routine part of business, and also provides an excellent opportunity to make a great first impression. The same ideas about defining your objective apply for receptions, as there is ample time to mingle about and network with both company representatives, customers, and other guests.

Think about who will be in attendance, and perhaps call the meeting organizer to see if a specific person is going to be there. With increased security at events these days, don't be surprised if they will not react favorably to your request, but it's worth a try. Hopefully you know the organizer (it helps). Explain that you would like to introduce yourself to them there, and are wondering if they are expected to attend. They may help you out, or not!

Again, ask yourself, "Is this the *best* place to meet this person?"

Your first task when attending a reception is to check-in at the registration table and get your nametag (to be worn on the right-hand side — above your handshaking hand — for easy viewing). Next, proceed into the room and step to the side. Avoid the "lost tourist" open-mouth look when entering a room. Enter with style and grace, with shoulders back and good posture. You know that people have a tendency to keep an eye on the door to see who is coming in – make the most of your entrance!

Sorry to be the bearer of party-pooper news, but don't head straight for the bar. First, find the event host, if possible, to thank them for inviting you. Next, scope out the room for the people you have in mind to meet. Once you are comfortable with the layout of the room, and where you might proceed next, go to the bar for your beverage (whew).

Usually it is easiest to approach a group of three or more, as one person can branch off to talk to you. When you approach a group, be ready to reach out with a handshake and introduce yourself. Wait for a break in the conversation or for someone to welcome you, but be ready!

When the shoe is on the other foot, be inclusive, not exclusive, when it comes to others approaching *you*. Begin by welcoming someone with a warm smile and eye contact, then stop the conversation to introduce yourself and welcome them to your conversation.

At a reception, keep your conversations to a limit of five minutes. Consider that everyone is there to meet and chat with as many people as possible.

How do you move from one conversation to another? Wait for a bit of a lull in the conversation, then simply say something like, "It's been wonderful talking with you this evening. I hope we run into each other again during the convention (if appropriate). Have a great evening!" And move on. It is perfectly acceptable to move to another conversation. It could be that the other person wants to move on as well.

Polishing your presence

AT RECEPTIONS

1. Avoid carbonated beverages if they tend to make you burp!

2. *Careful* is the word when it comes to alcoholic beverages. I make it a rule to only have one before dinner. None is fine as well.

3. Holding your drink in your left hand keeps your right hand dry and ready for handshaking.

4. Keep a linen handkerchief in your left-hand pocket for emergency sneezes. If one comes on, turn your head, quietly sneeze, then excuse yourself to blow your nose. Nose blowing is not something we do in public.

5. Keep your business cards in your right-hand pocket. Do not offer a business card every time you meet someone. In the United States, we appreciate having a bit of conversation before we exchange cards. However, if someone offers their card right away, follow their lead.

6. As mentioned before, keep your contact to handshaking only; refrain from hugging or otherwise touching people – it is not always appreciated!

7. Personally thank the representative from the host company or organization. Depending upon the event, a written thank you may also be a nice touch.

—— Chapter 12 ——
Taking Convention Guests for a Meal

One popular way to maximize your time with staff or clients at a convention is to invite them for dinner (usually lunch is part of the convention program and, in most cases, so is a dinner banquet, if not more than one). Check out your company policy on entertainment reimbursement, especially when it comes to hosting people from your own company. You don't want to embarrass yourself and others by having someone of a higher authority grab the check from your hand. Often company policy dictates that the person with the highest authority pays the check.

Think through who will be attending, from your own company and outside as well. Perhaps you want to invite members of your own company to dinner as a type of "teambuilding" event, or maybe your time would be better spent hosting customers. It could be that a combination of the two is the best option. Keep in mind that a convention often allows little free time, so take the convention agenda into consideration when planning invitations.

Often there is a "free night," and it could be that either members of your team or clients would really prefer going out with you than ordering room service. Also, don't consider only a dinner event. This is the time to let your creativity out. Maybe a show or sporting event after dinner would provide a much-needed entertainment break from the convention at hand, and help you promote your business as well.

If it isn't possible to host an entire meal and/or event, perhaps you could meet a client for coffee or a cocktail before a scheduled part of the convention, or you could ask them to join you at the actual convention meal. Often people attend conventions alone, and they would appreciate the invitation to dine or sit with you – especially if it is a huge gathering. They can be daunting!

With these ideas in mind, make sure to extend these invitations well before you arrive in a convention city. If you extend the invitation once on site (unless it is for an informal cup of coffee when you run into someone), you run the risk of giving the impression of a "last minute" invite! Your guests should feel pampered well before the trip.

Once in the convention city, leave a message at the person's hotel to confirm your arrangements. It is a nice touch to arrange for transportation for your guest; e.g., pick them up yourself in your own car or cab. If you have not shared the same transportation with your guests, arrange to meet them in the lobby of the hotel or restaurant in which you will be dining. Be very careful to give specific information about where you will meet! There is nothing worse than sitting in one part of a facility while your guests are waiting in another. It happens all of the time, especially when there may be two hotels of the same name in the same city.

Remember that the person who does the inviting does the paying, so you will be responsible for paying the tab, including the tip.

When it comes to paying the tab, a nice way to handle it is to discuss it with the host/hostess or server in advance and arrange to pay the tab at the end of the meal at the desk out front. This way, the tab is not brought to the table at all. Simply excuse yourself during the dessert course and take care of the tab – slick!

You may recall from an earlier chapter that the "host" of a meal has several responsibilities (see chapter 8). This is your time to shine! You are in charge, and everyone will be looking to you for timing (when you put your napkin in your lap, they will do so, etc.). You set the pace of the meal. Make sure to order all of the same courses as your guests, and pace your actual dining to everyone else so no one is left eating alone.

When hosting a meal at a convention, it could be that a member of your party will invite you for an impromptu "after dinner" cocktail afterwards. If this is the case, then allow them to pick up the check, as it is their invitation.

Polishing your presence

HOSTING A MEAL

1. Introduce yourself to the dining room host/hostess and head server so that it is clear that you are in charge of the party.

2. Do not remove your jacket – same goes for women and men. Your jacket is considered part of your outfit, and should be worn. I'm not talking about an overcoat, which should be hung away from the table, not folded over a chair.

3. Include everyone in the table conversation.

4. If you need to leave the table for *any* reason, simply say "excuse me." We don't need to know where you are going!

5. Smoking has truly gone by the wayside; I don't recommend leaving at any point during an event to smoke for many reasons, not the least of which is that you might come back smelling of smoke.

—— Chapter 13 ——
Tips on Tipping

It feels great to compliment others! And it's free! If a service employee does an exceptional job of anticipating and meeting your needs, saying an appreciative "thank you for the excellent service" goes a long way toward making their day. Don't forget the tip, of course!

A "gratuity" or "tip" is defined as a gift of money give for a service rendered. Interestingly, the acronym for T.I.P. is often defined as "to insure promptness" or "to insure prompt service." I like to think of good service as more inclusive than just promptness, as do most people. I judge the entire experience, from seating to smiles, and base my tip accordingly. However, a tip should never be considered "required." Although it is true that most wait staff, for example, depend upon tips to augment their salaries (often minimum wage), your tip should reflect their commitment to good service, and should not be expected for poor service.

To help insure good service, I have found that making eye contact and saying a warm "hello" or "good evening" to any service person at the outset helps with my entire experience. Everyone likes to be acknowledged and treated with respect, especially those who make their living serving others.

The calculation of a tip should not be discussed with your guests. The person paying the tip is obviously the person paying the check, and if you are someone's *guest* for a meal, you should not offer to pay the tip. I find this particularly embarrassing when I take someone for a meal, because while it seems a generous offer, if I were to accept, they would have to view the bill to calculate the tip! Ouch! I don't want my guests to see the bill, right? As previously mentioned, one cannot reciprocate for a gift during a gift (the meal), but rather should invite their host for a meal at a later date, or when traveling, perhaps invite them for an after-dinner drink in the bar or at another location.

Prepare yourself for tipping when traveling by having cash on-hand, and easily accessible. This can be particularly difficult for women who carry purses, so consider keeping some $1 and $5 bills handy in your coat pocket for the bellman, etc.

There are several websites available for your detailed tipping questions. From your hair stylist to golf caddy, understanding the appropriate amount can seem confusing. With a few simple clicks, prepare yourself for the event at hand, and take the guessing out of your next outing. In the meantime, here are a few general guidelines to get you started.

> A tip should be based on the pre-tax amount.

FINE DINING

1. Tip $20+ to the headwaiter / maitre d' (usually as you are about to be seated) to assure good seating and service for the evening. The amount varies depending upon the quality of the restaurant and how often you plan to dine there.

2. Tip the server 15%, 20% if it is an upscale restaurant or if you are hosting a large party (say 6 or more); however, read your check carefully. Often

a group gratuity is automatically added to a large party. You may add to that, if you desire.

3. Tip the wine steward 10-15% of the wine bill.

4. Tip the waiter $1 if he goes outside to call you a cab.

5. Tip $2-3 to the attendant or valet who brings your car around.

6. Tip $1 for each coat checked and $2 if you checked any shopping bags or umbrellas with your coat.

7. Tip $1 to the restroom attendant, $5 for services like sewing a button or removing a spot on a tie or gown.

FAST FOOD AND DELIVERY

You are not required to tip in a pizza parlor or deli, but if someone provides extra service in a cheerful manner, a $1-$2 tip is appropriate, especially if you are picking up a large order. Of course, it is expected that you would tip a pizza delivery person, usually 15% or more, depending upon the weather, difficulty parking at your house, etc.

HOTELS

1. Bags should be carried by the bellman. In a nice hotel, you should not carry even one small bag around, unless you are very late for a flight. Tip the bellman $3, or $1 per bag.

2. Tip the room service waiter 20% of bill, with a $2 minimum.

3. Tip the maid $2 per night (left on your pillow, so they know it is for them; a thank-you note is also much appreciated).

4. Tip $1 to $5 to the bellman who runs an errand for you, depending upon the time commitment.

5. Tip $1 to the doorman for getting you a cab.

6. Tip $2 to $5 to the doorman who goes out in inclement weather to get you a cab.

7. Tip $5 to a concierge who has provided extra-special service.

TAXIS AND LIMOUSINES

1. Tip 15% to taxi drivers, and 20% to limousine drivers.

2. Note: if you are caught in a traffic jam with a zone taxi driver (not paid by time), tip up to $5 more for his time. It is up to you, but if he complains through the whole incident, give him less!

3. Again, remember that tipping is not required. If you do not receive a smooth ride and gracious service, let it show in your tip!

AIRPORT

1. For curb-side check-in, tip $1 per bag.

2. For wheelchair service, tip $3-5 or more if it is a very long or complicated journey, or if you are provided excellent service.

3. For an electric cart ride, tip $3-5 or more depending upon the quality of service.

In addition, fill out a customer service response card or send a letter to the manager praising an exceptional employee by name and congratulating the manager on their wisdom in having this person on staff.

If the exceptional service happens in a restaurant your business frequents regularly, letters such as these – written on company letterhead – are often posted in the foyer. This helps build long-lasting customer relationships . . . and good service as well!

— *Part Seven* —
CORPORATE SPECIAL EVENTS

In the corporate arena, special events such as dinner banquets or golf outings are sometimes included as part of a corporate retreat, meeting or conference. Unfortunately, not everyone is comfortable in such situations! From the dance floor to the first tee, this section will help set the stage for an enjoyable event.

> *Some people wait so long for their ship to come in,*
> *their pier collapses. –John Goddard*

Here's what drives people crazy —

1. People I am traveling with don't have cash on hand for tipping.

2. My office *requires* everyone to participate in a sporting event.

3. My host doesn't tell me that a dance will be held as part of a business banquet.

4. No one mentions we won't be playing 'best ball' but rather regular golf.

5. I'm pushed to play golf when I don't know how to play!

6. The dress code for a team building event wasn't mentioned.

7. The music is so loud it is difficult to hold table conversation.

8. My dance partner's grip is too tight!

9. My dance partner's cologne is too strong! (Remember, cologne is not particularly appreciated at a corporate event.)

10. My dance partner does not walk me back to my chair.

11. I am the only one left at the table – help! Where did they go?

—— Chapter 14 ——
Prepare and Participate!

No matter what the occasion, do your homework. Half the challenge is in the preparation! When invited to special events, feel free to contact the event sponsor/host to check on special arrangements, such as appropriate dress, scheduling of the day and/or evening, etc. Of course you will RSVP! The sign of a true professional is someone who not only arrives on time, but RSVPs – giving the host notice whether you will attend. Some people mistakenly think that an RSVP is required only if you WILL attend an event; as a courtesy, a kind response is necessary either way.

If a phone call is encouraged, this would be a good time to ask specific questions about the event. For sporting activities, will you have access to a locker or dressing area? Exactly how is the game going to work? For example, a round of "best ball" is great fun in golf, as all four people on a team have a chance to play, then the "best ball" is chosen for the round. For people who don't know how to golf, this is a great way to include everyone, and also make sure everyone is having a good time.

The more information you have about where you will dress and shower, and whether you should bring your own lock, etc., the more comfortable you will be. Come prepared, and have fun!

As we do not have room in this book to cover all sports and events, may I just mention one sensitive item – cleaning up after ourselves. Whenever any sporting equipment or exercise machines are used, make sure to wipe them down for use by the next person. This pet peeve is mentioned to me often!

Chapter 15
Dancing Etiquette

It may seem old school, but dancing is still popular, especially for more formal events such as auctions and fundraisers. You may find yourself in the room representing your company or special interest charity, and avoiding the dance floor may leave you out in the cold when it comes to networking with friends and associates.

If you consider yourself clumsy on the dance floor, you are not alone! Most of us have not had the opportunity to learn to dance formally. I would like to suggest that if dancing is part of your professional life, give yourself the gift of a few dance lessons. Just like anything else, knowing the basics will help you get up from the table and join in the fun. With the onset of recent media, ballroom dancing is taking on a new popularity, and you may see it making a comeback at more conventions and events, not only in the form of a dance, but as dance lesson-type activities!

With the help of internationally known coach and competitor Natasha Thayer (www.easy2dance.com), here's a few things to keep in mind as you step onto the floor:

1. If you must decline a dance offer from someone, do not accept an offer during the same song from someone else.

2. Savvy dancers know that the "line of dance" is counter clockwise, generally speaking, although some types of dances allow you to pretty much stay in the same place. If you are moving, move counter clockwise, and watch out for the couple behind you!

3. Caution! When you step onto the dance floor, be careful not to disrupt the couples already dancing. Just like at a stop sign, stop and look before stepping out.

4. Caution again! When leaving the floor, be graceful but quick. Tradition calls for gentlemen to offer their arm and escort their partners back to the table – a nice touch! Do not keep your partner talking on the floor unless you have asked for the next dance. They may miss an opportunity to take another partner.

5. If you are an educated dancer, refrain from "showing" your partner how to do a step, unless they ask for assistance. The gentleman leads, of course, and the lady follows, but there is nothing more insulting than a man who stops dead in his tracks, and says, "watch this"!

6. Be careful not to block the entrance to the dance floor.

7. For politeness-sake, thank your partner at the end of a dance.

— Chapter 16 —
Golf Etiquette

Considering that I am not particularly golf savvy, and have experienced the embarrassment of attending corporate golf events without the proper preparation, I thought it would be a good idea to ask for some expert advice from my colleague, Mr. Golf Etiquette himself, Jim Corbett (www.mrgolf.com). Jim is the author of "The Pocket Idiot's Guide to Golf Rules and Etiquette."

"Business Golf for the New Golfer" By Jim Corbett, Mr. Golf Etiquette, Copyright 2008.

How wonderful! You've been invited to play golf in the company tournament! All the top executives will all be there, your direct bosses three levels up will all be there and all of those people below you who are trying to get your job will all be there too. Well, what a great opportunity to have some fun with your colleagues, spend a day away from the hubbub of the office and to get to know your co-workers in a totally new way.

What's that? You've never swung a golf club in your life and you fully expect this will be the ultimate career-limiting experience? Not to worry. You've seen golf on TV before, right? You've seen how easy it is for them, right? Really, the ball is NOT moving until you hit, so how hard could this possibly be? I mean Tiger Woods, Phil Mickelson, Annika Sorenstam – what have they got that you haven't got? – besides gazillions of dollars and a clue?

Not to worry. You have a secret weapon that will help you to carry the day in style, and could have you eating in the executive dining room by the end of the week. But first, let's go through the checklist of necessities.

Okay, first: Do you have golf clubs? No? No problem. You can borrow some or get some on e-bay (be careful with e-bay because the ones you find there might not work too well — either that or the previous owner probably wouldn't be selling them on e-bay). But if you need them right away rent a set at your local pro shop.

How about golf balls? Buy a dozen or so just to be careful. Chances are you won't hit them far enough to lose them, but it is always better to be safe than sorry. And while you're buying those, ask the pro shop staff to help you with some other incidentals like a glove, some tees and those kind of things. They'll be happy to make the sale and you'll feel much better about the game of golf – at least you're shopping.

Then take a quick lesson from a pro at the local golf course. This won't help you to become a great golfer, but at least you'll understand how many different levels you're failing on. Ha! Only kidding. Taking a lesson will give you some fundamentals about stance, grip and the basic elements of the swing – the backswing, hitting the ball and the follow-through.

Okay, here are a few useful terms for you to practice before you show up at the big event:

Par – the recommended number of strokes for any given hole. (i.e., a short hole is a Par-3, an average length hole is a Par-4 and a long hole is a Par-5.) Sample usage: *I sure wish I had gotten at least one par on any hole today.*

Birdie – One less than Par on a hole (i.e., a score of 2 on a Par-3). Sample usage: *Do you mind if I eat these extra crispy potato chips while you putt for that birdie?*

Bogey – One more than Par on a hole (i.e., a score of 5 on a Par-4). Sample usage: *Was that steam I saw coming out of your ears after you missed that 2-foot birdie putt and ended up with a Bogey?*

Triple Bogey – Three more than Par on a hole (i.e., a score of 7 on a Par-4). Sample usage: *That's amazing, you threw your putter farther than you hit your drive when you made that triple bogey.*

That should cover you for the day; don't worry, you'll pick up a few other very colorful expressions while you're out on the golf course.

Okay, first it is important to note that in a corporate event you are probably going to be playing a "best ball" tournament. That means that everyone will hit a shot and the next shot will be hit from the place where the best of those first shots landed. That's perfect for you because if you hit a lousy shot you get to pick it up and put it where everyone else is. See how easy this is going to be?

Here is a killer strategy that you can employ to drive them all crazy. Are you ready? Okay, here it is: Have fun!

If you are playing poorly and still having fun it will make everyone wonder how you are doing it and they will think you understand the deepest mysteries of the universe. And in fact, you do.

But after all is said and done, the thing that will get you through the day and make you a hero is the new golfer's best friend. And that secret weapon is Golf Etiquette.

Golf etiquette is the system of rituals and courtesies that golfers – even new ones – extend to one another that can turn a really bad game of golf into... well, into a really bad game of golf with good manners.

Let's look at a few of the basic rules of golf etiquette that you can use to get through your round of golf so that you look like a pro, even though you might not hit the ball very well. A few of these rules apply everywhere on the golf course and a few are specific to when you are on the green. Remember these rules and your playing partners will be delighted to have you around any time.

General Rules of Golf Etiquette

1. Quiet when someone is hitting or putting.

2. Stay out of their peripheral vision.

3. Make sure your shadow is also out of view.

4. Repair what you have disturbed (i.e., replace divots, rake sand traps, repair ball marks).

5. Be ready when it is your turn and don't delay the pace of the game.

6. Watch how the more experienced golfers do it – and do it like them.

7. Remember that golf is a game! Smile and have fun!

Golf Etiquette Rules on the Green

1. Watch out for other people's golf balls.

2. Don't step on the path along which they are about to putt.

3. Take your golf ball out of the hole right after you sink a putt.

4. When you take your ball out of the hole, don't step on or near the hole.

5. Keep your golf cart away from the green.

Follow the simple steps outlined above and your day will be an unparalleled success. At the end of the day your rivals will be undone, your superiors will be impressed, and your career will experience the meteoric rise it has always deserved.

And don't throw away the business card of that teaching pro; you may want to start planning now to get ready for next year!

── Part Eight ──
OFFICE ETIQUETTE

Consider this: in an office setting, you spend more than 40 hours per week with people you have not chosen to spend time with, may not have a thing in common with, have different personalities than you, have different beliefs and morals, and perhaps have personal habits that may be, well, annoying. This may be more time than you spend with your family and friends! In most cases, we do not work in a vacuum and in most organizations, it is all about the team. No matter what your experience or education, your ability to work with others can make the difference between success or failure, and it all begins with office etiquette. You knew I was going to say that.

Before we talk about specifics, keep in mind that every office has its own protocol, or chain of command. It is a good idea to clarify your office protocol as soon as you join a company. Nothing can jeopardize your

> *Know yourself. Don't accept your dog's admiration as conclusive evidence that you are wonderful. –Ann Landers*

office relationships faster than going over someone's head or otherwise not observing appropriate office protocol.

It will be worth your while to quickly review the following "pet peeves" supplied by my clients over the past few years. This is a rare opportunity to find out what is really driving people crazy. What is the most popular complaint? It drives people crazy when . . . someone walks right into their office or office space without announcing themselves, and then stands there waiting until they are off the phone or finished talking with someone else. A tip: when someone is on the phone or has someone else in their office, come back later! My apologies if some of these are a bit graphic. Enjoy these and the rest which appear throughout the book, all comments from actual folks who are definitely frustrated! Let's get started.

Here's what's driving people crazy –

1. People don't say "please" and "thank you."

2. My work associates discuss religion in the workplace.

3. My work associates spend too much time chatting with customers when we are really busy (if we aren't busy, it's okay)!

4. People talk so fast it is hard to understand them.

5. People talk on cell phones in restroom stalls and in public lines, such as at the grocery store or bank.

6. People eat while they are talking on the phone, especially at their desk.

7. People INTERRUPT all the time!

8. People slam or drop the phone in your ear when they hang up.

9. My work associates miss deadlines.

10. My office team won't pitch in and answer the phones.

11. People I am meeting with interrupt our talk to answer the phone.

12. People talk too loudly in the office.

13. A conference call is placed on speaker phone in an open office landscape.

14. E-mails are sent to people who are not involved in a project.

15. People do not wear deodorant.

16. My workmates take care of personal business on company time.

17. People chew gum in the workplace.

18. People are constantly negative.

19. My associates don't ask me if I have time to visit before launching into a conversation.

— *Chapter* 17 —
Professional Manners
Where do you stand?

Do you view yourself as a leader? Do others? First impressions are everything. From the moment you walk into a room, you are saying something about yourself, whether or not you open your mouth. Everything about you — from the polish on your shoes to the way you carry yourself — says "leader." Picture someone in your life that you respect and admire. How do they carry themselves?

Walk tall, with your head held high. Look around a room with dignity. Hold your arms at your sides — keep your hands still, and do not put them in your pockets. Do not adjust your clothing or mess with your hair (hair flippers beware). Stand straight, with shoulders back. Wear comfortable shoes that are polished and clean. Do not wear "sexy" shoes or other distracting clothing.

How is your grammar and word usage? A third grade teacher was trying to teach her class grammar: "You should never say, "I seen him do it," she told her class. "Yeah," piped up a voice from the back of the room . . . "especially if you ain't sure he done it." Speak clearly and distinctly, use good grammar, make strong eye contact – then listen. Show you care by listening with heart.

OFFICE BEHAVIOR CHECK-UP

Not me! I never do that! It's time for your annual office behavior check-up. Few people have the luxury of an office with a door, so it's time to check-in to see how your office behavior is affecting your neighbors at work. The trick is to put privacy first in an open office environment.

Check these out:

1. Sound travels. Keep your voice down and talk into your "back-bar" or partition in your space, not out into an open area.

2. When you approach someone's office space, announce yourself. A simple, "Hello, Jack" will do. Stand at the "virtual door" until invited to enter. Ask the person if they have a minute to talk to you or whether they would like to schedule an appointment. Do not sit down unless you are offered a chair. My clients frequently complain to me about people who come into their office, plop down and chat about personal business – all without being invited. How do they ask them to leave without hurting their feelings? I suggest standing up to greet the person. This is strong body language that you do not want the person to sit down. Stay standing, and say something to the effect that while you would love to be able to chat right now, you are unable to, and ask if they would like to set up a time later in the day.

3. Don't look over someone's shoulder when they are working on the computer. Likewise, do not listen to telephone conversations – step back. "Announce" yourself in an open office atmosphere by saying "Good morning" or "Hello" to let people know you are standing behind them or entering their office space.

4. It's not a good idea to begin business conversations in the rest room or in public hallways! I cannot believe the number of times someone has actually followed me into the restroom to talk to me. If this happens to you, stop outside of the restroom to finish the conversation. Do not go in if someone is chatting with you. If the conversation goes on, simply

excuse yourself and ask if you can finish the conversation later in the day.

5.   Jokes are inappropriate in the workplace. Please do not interpret laughter as an acceptance of a joke. In etiquette, it is considered rude to make others feel uncomfortable; thus, you will not be told if your joke is offending or hurting someone. This does not mean to lose your sense of humor, just "joke telling." Often jokes are centered around making fun of people or a group of people – totally inappropriate in the workplace.

6.   People really do not want to hear details about illness or disease, personal relationships, pregnancy, child rearing, etc., in the workplace. Again, they may not tell you, but wouldn't it be nicer to talk about something else?

7.   Also, do not ask people personal questions such as whether they are married, have children, how long they have been married, etc. These topics are considered very personal, and are off limits unless the person brings up the topic themselves; e.g., if someone mentions their children's soccer game you could ask how long they have been involved or whatever, or where they play, etc.

8.   And what is the most mentioned pet peeve? Perfume and cologne. Simply, save the scents for personal enjoyment, away from the workplace. Even scented body lotion can be too strong for the office. I recommend baby powder ONLY at work.

WHAT IS YOUR WORD USAGE SAYING ABOUT YOU?

It's amazing how words can define us. From how we utter them to which words we choose, proper language sets the stage for how we are viewed professionally. A leader may know how to dress, how to walk, and how to shake hands properly, but if words are misused, misunderstanding follows making successful communication a constant challenge.

In today's world, spell check may rule, but it cannot save you from yourself when it comes to the spoken word. And, we may be blundering away on a regular basis without a clue. I agree with Ann Landers, "Know yourself! Don't accept your dog's admiration as conclusive evidence that you are wonderful."

Our dogs may love us anyway, but your coworkers may not appreciate our misuse of words. How do we improve our grammar? By reading, listening and writing. It might feel like homework, but it can be an exciting journey. Picking up the works of great authors helps with creativity, and listening to great speakers opens up a whole new world when it comes to delivery – if we are paying attention. A good beginning. For me, the best exercise is to write and then write it again with help from of a variety of reference books. I also keep a list of words that tend to be confusing – or confused! Here's a few to get your list going. Test these at your next staff meeting or at the family dinner table, and see what you discover:

Among or **between**? Choose *among* when you are choosing between <u>more</u> than two options, *between* when it is two.

Amount or **number**? Use *amount* when you are referring to the bulk or sum total of something, such as water or soil; use *number* when you are referring to something that can be counted, such as number of people.

Can or **may**? Use *can* when you are asking if someone has the ability to do something, such as "Can she speak German?" Use *may* when you are asking permission, "May I help you?"

Farther or **further**? Chose *farther* when you are talking about physical distance that can be measured, such as miles; use *further* when it is something that cannot be measured, like further study.

Fewer or **less**? Use *fewer* when items can be counted, such as people; use *less* when items cannot be counted, such as water.

Irregardless is actually an unacceptable version of "regardless." Use the word "regardless."

Inappropriate Language

I have mentioned inappropriate language in the conversation section of this book, but I am compelled to mention it again with regard to office etiquette. One way to "put people off" is to use inappropriate language such as swearing, especially in an office environment where you are seeing the same people every day. Given what is acceptable in the media these days, I am not surprised at what young people are picking up as appropriate, but it is simply inappropriate when it seeps into the office environment. While this language may be considered appropriate in casual situations by some – I beg to differ. It can upset the success of a social engagement as readily as a business one. I'm sure you know what words I'm talking about, so I won't go into detail, but one I should mention is the use of "you guys." Please avoid it. Simply refer to a group as "you." Also, please use "men" and "women," not "boys" and "girls."

OFFICE GIFT GIVING: WHO CARES?

Selecting the perfect gift should be a joy, not a chore, whether for friends or workmates. Giving someone a gift should take great thought and care, from the gift itself to the presentation.

First, check out your office policy for gift giving, and stay the course within those guidelines. The good news is — it is not necessary for you to purchase a gift for your boss or supervisor, unless you have been working for them for a very long time and have a good working relationship. Even then, if you desire to give a gift, it should be a small one, such as a box of chocolates or specialty coffee. Sometimes a group of people will "chip in" for a gift for the boss. Often this causes pressure on people to contribute when, as I mentioned, it is not necessary to purchase a gift for the boss. A special toast from the staff at a holiday function accompanied by a very nice card personally signed by all of the staff involved would be a good alternative.

However, it is appropriate for the boss to select gifts for his or her staff. This could come in the form of a nice luncheon or outing. This gift should be considered separate from any kind of official year-end bonus, which is not the same as a holiday gift.

Presentation is everything! Take the time to wrap your gift with care and present it from your heart. A gift should be given in person, not left on someone's desk — a warm smile and handshake from the boss is much appreciated.

What about your workmates? It is not necessary to purchase gifts for everyone in your department; however, sometimes people enjoy bringing cookies or something to share. If you exchange gifts with a personal friend from work, please do so away from the office.

If you are invited to a holiday office party at someone's home, remember to bring a host/hostess gift – a flower arrangement (not cut flowers), a basket of fruit, or a bottle of wine or box of chocolate.

Finally, please be sensitive to the fact that we all do not celebrate the same holidays. Refrain from giving gifts that represent a particular holiday. Gifts should represent your careful thought, and NOT display a company or department logo!

Who cares about gift giving? You. And your gifts show it.

PERSONAL CELL PHONES

The popularity and convenience of cell phone use has created a new chapter in the world of business etiquette. There is a difference between a personal cell phone and a work cell phone, which is an important distinction in the office! Some people have need for a cell phone on the job, others don't. No matter which situation, cell phones should not be used for personal business in the office. If the phone is part of your job, make sure to mute it during business meetings, and unless you have an emergency-related position, try to avoid looking at it to distraction when it buzzes in your pocket. Consider it the same situation as when someone is meeting with you in your office – proper manners dictate that you should not answer a phone call when someone is talking with you in your office (unless you have an emergency role within an organization). The exception to this is that if you know you are expecting an important emergency phone call, let folks know in advance that you may have to excuse yourself from the meeting.

OFFICE CHAT

People are often surprised when I talk about how it is impolite to converse with business associates about their health. This falls within the category of "personal" business, and is inappropriate, whether business or personal. While it is acceptable to say "how are you?" it is not acceptable to ask about a recent surgery or compliment someone on a weight loss; after all, weight loss is not always a good thing.

It is also inappropriate to comment on someone's physical beauty. This also falls under the "personal" category, and can be misinterpreted (let's not get into the ramifications regarding sexual harassment.) As always, I recommend finding other things to compliment people on, such as a project they have recently completed or a special presentation. People prefer being complimented on their work, not their looks. I would much rather have you tell me that you enjoyed one of my speeches, not that you liked my outfit!

Accepting compliments with style and grace is another sign of professionalism. It always amazes me how people are so eager to dismiss a compliment. Simply saying "thank you" is the best response to a compliment. Do not dismiss a compliment by saying something like, "Oh, this suit? I haven't worn it in ages and wasn't sure it would fit." Simply thank the person for the gift of the compliment.

SHOULD WOMEN OPEN DOORS FOR MEN?

Absolutely! While men have been conditioned from a very early age to open the door for women, the appropriate protocol would be for a woman to wait for a moment for the man to open the door; if he doesn't, she should open it and hold it open for the man. She should also step up to the plate faster if the man is carrying boxes. Men, please don't run up behind a woman to open the door unless you want mace in the face; simply say, "May I get that door for you?" as you are walking behind her.

ELEVATOR ETIQUETTE – YES!

Here's the word on what should happen when entering and exiting elevators. First, when waiting for an elevator, stand back. There's nothing more rude than standing right in front of the door so that the people who are trying to exit have to blast through you before they can get out. Then, if there are men present, they should allow the women to enter first. I realize this goes counter to what I have been saying about men and women being equal when it comes to business etiquette; however, someone has to go through the door first! When exiting an elevator, the person closest to the door should simply get out. It is very awkward if men try to hold the door, etc., for people exiting an elevator. You are off the hook – simply get out!

Polishing your presence

IN THE OFFICE

1. Keep in mind that customers and clients may see you in your workplace parking lot. It's embarrassing to be seen smoking in your car, putting on makeup or yelling at someone on the cell phone in your car, let alone when the boss or a client is walking by.

2. When visiting someone else's office, wait to be offered a place to sit. Some people make themselves "at home" in other people's offices. This is often unwelcome!

3. Do not chew gum in the office.

4. Eating at your desk may or may not be against company policy, but I recommend dining away from your desk. Not only do you appear unprofessional when dining, you are seen as "available" to do business, and what if you answer a business call with a mouthful of spaghetti? You deserve – and need – the break. Take it!

5. Sound travels. Your neighbor might not appreciate the radio station you are listening to or your favorite CD, no matter how quiet you have it – and remember, even if you ask them if it is bothering them, they are unlikely to admit it for fear of upsetting you.

6. I'm not quite sure how to explain this clearly to you, but perhaps the best way is to call it amenable. Those who are flexible and open to other people's ideas are the most appreciated co-workers. Those who argue at the drop of a hat or make a "big deal" over a simple situation are not. Choose your battles – picking a restaurant for lunch or type of coffee served at meeting should not be at the top of your list.

— Chapter 18 —
Internationally Speaking

Those who work in international business understand very well the importance of appropriate etiquette and polished manners. Unlike in the United States, where attitudes regarding informal social graces are becoming uncomfortably common and "acceptable," it is not the case internationally. Business people are left with heads spinning when business deals go bad due to social gaffes because, as I mentioned earlier, it most probably will never be explained that they did not shake the hand of everyone in a room, or ignored the spouse or guest of a business partner.

The best advice I can convey is to study up BEFORE doing business with other countries. It's too late if you're stopping by the book store on the way to the airport. Rest assured that internationals spend the required time studying up on our business protocol, and we should honor them the same way. I suggest that you take advantage of the internet to familiarize yourself in international protocol.

Here's what's driving people crazy –

1. People act as if the "American Way" is the only way to do something.

2. People ignore those from other countries, rather than try to start up a conversation.

3. My work associates give an international person an easy-to-pronounce "nickname" rather than learn how to pronounce their name correctly.

4. People make rude comments about other cultures.

5. People make assumptions about someone's homeland based on their appearance.

First, understand that you should honor the protocol and etiquette of the country in which you are traveling. Likewise, visitors to the United States will honor our protocol. This is why it is extremely important for us to educate ourselves on our OWN practices, as internationals are well versed in what is appropriate here.

Know everything you can about the countries you will be working with in order to avoid sensitivities.

Keep in mind that in many countries, business is not done over a meal. Rather, mealtime is a time to get to know each other personally. In some cases, it would be considered rude to bring up business at all.

Research the form of greeting for the country in which you will be traveling, and practice it carefully. And, while English may be the default language in many cases, speak slowly and clearly, and be prepared to repeat yourself. Americans are known for speaking too quickly. Often your point will simply be lost, as not every culture will ask you to repeat yourself.

If you are working with an interpreter, make eye contact with the person you are communicating with, not the interpreter. It can be awkward, but you will get used to it.

Americans are often thought of as "know it alls." Keep your point of view to yourself until you have listened carefully to all sides. Generally speaking, be culturally sensitive to others' points of view and accepting that there are more ways to do things than you may have considered.

Polishing your presence

INTERNATIONALLY

1. Make detailed plans for meetings and meals before you travel. Outside of the U.S. you cannot just pick up the hotel room phone and set appointments; it is considered presumptuous and rude.

2. Status is particularly important to executives outside of the U.S. and Canada. Here, the CEO of a major corporation could be on a first-name basis with a mail room attendant. Not so abroad! If you are a Vice President, you will be meeting with the same level executive, and should not request to meet with anyone above that level.

3. Instant familiarity is not appreciated internationally; you will cause discomfort if you call new acquaintances by their first names, or if you invite them to call you by your first name.

4. Introductions are critically important. Remember that the highest ranking executive's name is spoken first: "Mr. Senior Executive, may I present Mr. Junior Executive." Then provide additional information . . . "Mr. Junior Executive represents our West Coast Sales Office." This will help the more senior person start a conversation. Of course, the client is always number one!

— *Part Nine* —
HIGH TECH ETIQUETTE TUNE-UP

So far, we've been focusing on building relationships in person and, of course, much of our communication takes place over the phone or via e-mail. Unfortunately, it is impossible to convey a complete message without the benefit of seeing someone's facial expressions or, in the case of e-mails, not even being able to hear their voice. This is why we need to be so careful when not meeting in person. Always remembering that there is an actual person at the end of that voice mail message or computer screen is the first step.

> *Man's self-concept is enhanced*
> *when he takes responsibility for himself. –Unknown*

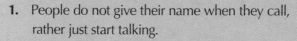

Here's what's driving people crazy —

1. People do not give their name when they call, rather just start talking.

2. People do not return phone calls in a timely manner.

3. My workmates answer personal cell phones at work, and I am treated to very personal conversations.

4. People speak too loudly in an open office landscape.

5. My associates spend time text messaging during meetings.

6. My e-mails go unanswered, leaving me wondering how to proceed.

7. My kind e-mails are answered in a curt and hurtful manner.

8. People call me to see if I received their e-mails sent within a few hours.

9. People do not include their phone numbers and addresses on their e-mail signatures.

10. People forward my e-mails to others without asking my permission.

— *Chapter* 19 —
Telephone and Cell Phone Etiquette

So much business is done on the telephone, it is wise to review your telephone skills. Some people actually place a mirror in their office so they can focus on that all-important "smile factor" during phone conversations. You'd be surprised how others can "hear" your smile!

Want to earn your associates' respect and loyalty? Return telephone calls on-time, speak slowly and clearly, and always thank people for their time.

A name is everything! Do you know how to pronounce the name of the person you are calling? Everyone likes to hear the sound of their own name, when spoken correctly! If you cannot figure out how to pronounce it, call the receptionist in the company to ask. Tell them the truth – that you are about to call someone in their organization and you would appreciate their help with the pronunciation of their name.

Especially outside of your company, use "Mr. and Ms." (honorifics) until people invite you to call them by their first name. By the way, we never use honorifics for ourselves . . . I would never say, "Hello, this is Ms. Horton." I would say, "Hello, this is Stephanie Horton," then the person on the other end would say, "Hello Ms. Horton." I realize that this sounds a bit formal for today's world, but remember, using honorifics (Mr. or Ms.) is a sign of respect and class, and you will be remembered for it.

Identify yourself immediately when making a call. Do not assume the person will recognize your voice. Say, "Good morning/afternoon, Mr. or Ms. Green, this is Joe Brown from Perfection Bank." After they say hello, determine if they have time to talk to you. Say, "Is this a good time to talk?" or "Do you have a few minutes?" If they say they have five minutes, keep your conversation to five minutes.

Consider the other person's schedule when deciding when to place a call. Avoid calling just before lunch or at the very end of the day, when they may be preparing to leave. Acknowledge how busy your client is, and how much you appreciate their taking the time to talk to you.

Use your best voice. Record your voice on your own voice mail to check out the sound of your own words. Make sure you speak in a clear, concise, and easy-sounding voice – not too loud, too soft or too fast. Are you easily understood? And, when leaving messages, always mention the specific reason for your call and the best time to reach you.

Be brief. Remember, many people check their messages via a cell phone and they may not have your number with them, so leave it again. When you leave your phone number, speak slowly and distinctly. (To be sure you are speaking at the proper pace, write your phone number as you leave it.)

If you are having trouble connecting with someone, set up a phone meeting at a time that would be convenient for them.

Just as you would when talking with anyone, be sure to treat receptionists and administrative staff with the utmost respect. Be patient – these positions often require an extreme balancing act of phone calls and visitors. They will appreciate – and remember – your kindness. However, do not engage in inappropriate conversation with the assistant, such as "Has Mr. Brown received my message?" or "What did he/she think of my proposal?" Keep your conversation to leaving a message. If the assistant asks why you are calling, you can say that you are following up on your recent meeting or packet you sent in the mail.

In the global marketplace, miscommunication is easier than ever. Speak slowly and clearly. Don't rush your conversation or say you understand something when you don't. Resist the urge to shout. Avoid slang or casual expressions that could be confusing or misunderstood. If necessary, make arrangements for an interpreter or a way to communicate in a written form. It is sometimes a good idea to follow your phone conversation with a letter or e-mail stating the next steps or decisions that have been made.

Cell Phone Etiquette

Cell phones have made quite an entrance into our business and personal lives, and are – honestly – starting to really irritate people! Unfortunately, the irritation comes from people forgetting either where they are and/or who may be listening to their conversation. Choosing an inappropriate time to have a cell phone conversation would be like inviting your parent on a date. The key is to think it through and go back to our original rule: would talking on the cell phone at this particular moment make someone uncomfortable? Embarrass someone (even you?) Ruin someone else's private dinner date or important business meeting? If we simply respect other people's space and time, common sense should rule.

For example, avoid bringing a cell phone to a business lunch or date unless you are expecting an urgent call. In this case, explain that you may be receiving the call and excuse the interruption. When the call comes through, go to the lobby or outside to take the call.

Do not use a cell phone in a public place where your conversation could disturb others, as we tend to speak louder on the cell phone than we would normally. If it is a must, find a private spot to chat.

Here's another pet peeve some people have mentioned – just because you are in the mall or in your car, do not ask others to do your work for you because they are in the office. In other words, don't ask others to look up things on your calendar, find files, etc., unless is it absolutely necessary. If

123

you know you are going to be making calls on the road, take the necessary backup information with you.

A final thought: what about text messaging? The considerations remain the same – if text messaging is going to take your attention away from the meeting or people at hand, or disturb them in any way, please refrain. The mere act of text messaging can be an annoyance to others as they will assume – rightly so – that they do not have your full attention.

— Chapter 20 —
E-Mail Etiquette

Computers tend to be impersonal enough without letting technology erode your good manners, then business relationships. One of the biggest pet peeves arises from the type of communication itself. Most people don't realize that you should use the same medium as the person who has contacted you; e.g., if someone calls you, call them back. If someone sends you an e-mail, respond via e-mail. They may not have both available to them at the time. And remember, if you are leaving a message, ALWAYS leave your phone number. The person may be checking voice mail from a remote location. Here are a few tips for engaging, not alienating, communications:

If you are starting a project or a new working relationship with someone, establish guidelines about communications. Do they prefer e-mail? Or would they rather have you set up an appointment? Talk it through.

For ease in responding and filing messages, address one topic per message, and list the topic clearly in the subject line. People will also appreciate BRIEF e-mail messages! Keep it short and sweet!

Begin your messages with a "Dear Mr. Brown" (or first name, if you have established that kind of relationship) or "Hello Sam" — and end with a thank you and your name. Preferably, include your phone number, department, and other information just as you would on letterhead — every time! They may print out your message and take it on the road.

Don't use e-mail to communicate about sensitive or confidential matters, such as personnel issues or confidential contract information. Your e-mail messages may never be deleted. They can be forwarded, copied, stored and then retrieved at the most inconvenient times!

Use upper and lower case letters for easy reading. All caps indicates you are YELLING. And, avoid decorative stationery backgrounds, cartoons, etc. in business e-mail communications. Be careful when using the "reply all" button. Don't respond to everybody unless you mean to!

Angry or upset? STOP! As in any communications, sleep on it – everything will look better tomorrow . . . or at least different. In this case, consider responding with a meeting or telephone call.

Keep it appropriate. Don't send jokes in the workplace, gossip or talk about others via e-mail. Use your best grammar and avoid inappropriate language.

Don't cry wolf. Is it really urgent? Give plenty of response time for your messages; you should not expect immediate replies. While we should be checking our e-mail inbox two-three times a day, some people may be out of the office (of course, if you have it, use the "out of office" message). If someone hasn't returned your message, resist the temptation to follow them to the restroom with your question!

Polishing your presence

IN HIGH-TECH LAND

1. Keep in mind that we are always communicating with another human being, no matter what the communication method.

2. Your voice and written communications represent you – do you come off as professional and friendly or sharp and unapproachable?

3. Stay tuned to your technology; there's nothing more frustrating than working with people who have difficulty with technology. For example, know how to send and open attachments and photographs. Learn how to text message. Try your best to stay up with the technology.

4. Do not eavesdrop on others' conversations or e-mailing. If someone is working on the computer, announce yourself – do not come up behind them. They may think you are reading their e-mails.

5. Your signature footer should contain: name, position and department, organization, e-mail address, regular address, and phone/fax.

— *Part Ten* —
LOOKING THE PART

While it may not be true that "we are what we wear," it certainly can seem like it in a business setting. In an increasingly casual culture, business dress has unfortunately been kicked to the curb. I say "unfortunately" because I truly believe we are doing ourselves – and our companies – a disservice by not knowing how to dress appropriately in the office. Many of my clients have been basically forced to instigate dress codes to ward off the most obvious of dress nightmares, such as miniskirts and tank tops. Dress reflects not only on your own professionalism, but that of the company you represent. If your company has a dress code, study up! And, if not, hopefully the following tips will help. And, there are many books and websites devoted strictly to business dress.

> *Good business leaders create a vision,*
> *articulate the vision, passionately own the vision,*
> *and relentlessly drive it to completion. –Jack Welch*

Here's what's driving people crazy –

1. Someone in the office wears so much perfume, it is hard to sit in a meeting room with them.

2. Female workmates wear flip-flops into the office.

3. Management does nothing to enforce a company dress code.

4. A business associate compliments people on clothing in a personal manner.

5. When one can see a woman's undergarments underneath her clothing.

— Chapter 21 —
Business Casual Confusion

Dress in the workplace has become increasingly complicated! In the quest for appropriate business casual, even well-dressed executives are sometimes left out in the cold. Business dress traditionally means a business suit, for both men and women, but what exactly is business casual?

To get a clear picture, first define "business clothing" as formal, constructed tailored suits in dark and neutral colors, with light-colored shirts; don't forget the tie! And, on the other hand, define "casual clothing" as the relaxed, loose-fitting and colorful pieces you might wear at home or shopping, complete with tennis shoes or sandals.

"Business casual" really has nothing to do with casual clothing. It may be slightly more casual than traditional business dress, but is still for business, not the tennis court. The trick is to keep the professional look, and not go too far into the comfort zone! An example of business casual would be khaki pants (pressed), with a crisp shirt and sports jacket, still with a tie. Essentially, business casual is one slight cut below business dress — keep the iron hot!

An exception would be if you are attending a sports event or convention, then look for the dress code among the registration materials. When in doubt, ask!

Over-the-top wear would include things like halter tops, miniskirts, see-through blouses or sandals without socks. Anything that shows too much skin is definitely a *fashion don't* at work. The same goes for excessive jewelry, accessories and piercings. Shorts would also be in this category, as would Capri pants and strappy sandals without hose, even with a good pedicure! No offense, but we don't want to see your toes in a business atmosphere – keep them hidden until after work.

If your organization has a clear dress code, you are already one step ahead of the game. Having such a policy makes it easier for managers to coach employees who may be tempted to get a bit too comfortable, especially during the summer months.

Confused? My rule is this: always dress for the job you want, not the job you have. Take the guesswork out of your next promotion by putting yourself "in the picture" now! By dressing the part, management will already see you in your next role. And, clothing can affect your attitude! Why not look good and feel good every day?

When you're putting the final touches on your outfit, please remember to leave the perfume or cologne at home. It's not appreciated by your workmates, especially those who are allergic.

Details count. Make no mistake that your polished shoes, matching belt, beautiful briefcase and purse are noticed. They are. And, did you know that it is considered bad form to put a purse or briefcase onto a meeting table or especially someone's desk? Purses should go under your chair (at a meal as well), and the briefcase should also be placed under or near your chair. This is why it may be better to carry a leather folder with only the materials you will need for a meeting with you – this can be placed on the table.

Shoes should be well cared for and beautifully shined. Keep one of those instant shoe-shine buffers in your car or briefcase for emergencies A felt marking pen also works wonders for emergency fixes on the heels of black shoes. Make no mistake, your shoes ARE noticed. Always wear hose, and no toe viewing in business!

Keep jewelry to a minimum; most people don't realize how painful a handshake can be if a person is wearing a ring on their right hand, especially one with a high-set stone. Wear simple earrings, necklaces and bracelets – nothing that will distract from your conversation by making noise or dangling. Also a good watch will serve you well as professional jewelry.

Hairstyles change with the style, but conservative is the way to go for the workplace. Trendy styles – again – may serve as a distraction, not attraction. Be especially wary of styles that cause your hair to droop down over your eyes, or styles that cause you to flip your hair. It's amazing the fidgeting people do with their hair; it can definitely be distracting.

But what if it's a PARTY? I know. I hear this all the time. I hate to be the party pooper in the crowd, but I must advise – again – to be conservative in business wear, even if it is a party. Think about all the great work you have done so far to make a great impression. We don't want it to fall by the wayside when you show up in a cocktail dress better suited for an episode of "Sex in the City." Business is business, even if it is a "social" type event, so dress up but not to the point of distraction. One exception here would be shoes. For the women in the crowd, fancier shoes are acceptable for a cocktail event, as are dresses. Just be careful not to cross the plunging neckline line, or wear something too short or wispy, if you know what I mean.

Men's clothing for the business social event are pretty much the same as during the business day; however, if you wanted to zip it up a bit with a more colorful shirt and tie, that would be great. I still don't recommend cologne – for any business function. I'm no fun.

Casual Friday

It will probably come as no surprise to you that I'm not a big fan of casual Fridays, with the exception of a "logo" day or team sport day, which features clothing that functions more like a uniform (common in banking or retail). At work, observe the policies of your particular company when it comes to casual Friday. However, when visiting other companies, do NOT assume it is appropriate for you to dress down. Always dress the way you would when you visit any business account, first class.

Why don't I care for casual Friday? In my opinion, the way employees dress is a direct reflection upon the company, especially if they are receiving clients on-site. Clients, especially those from other countries, could easily misinterpret a "dress-down" day as a lack of respect or professionalism.

Informal

Before six o'clock, "informal" means a daytime-type dress or dressy suit for women and a coat and tie for men. After six-o'clock, women may wear a dressy afternoon dress or cocktail dress (short or long) or a suit. Men may wear either a light or dark business suit with a tie. Note: nylons or socks are required!

Formal

Before six o'clock, "formal" means a late afternoon dress or suit for the women and a dark suit for the men. After six o'clock: either black tie or white tie.

Black tie

Black tie means a long or short evening dress or evening wear separates for women. Gloves are optional. Remove your right-hand glove for receiving lines, remove both gloves for dining and drinking. For men, a single- or double-breasted dinner jacket or tuxedo with a black silk bow tie.

White tie

White tie is full evening dress! For women, wear your dressiest long gown. For men, wear a long black tailcoat and white bow tie or equivalent military uniform.

If you are in charge of an event, it is up to you to let your guests know the appropriate dress. If you are a guest, and the style of dress is not noted on the invitation, it is your responsibility to call the host or hostess for advice.

Polishing your Presence

THE LOOK

Here's a personal topic for you – underwear. My mother taught me well in this area. Spare no expense when it comes to undergarments, from your socks or hose up. For women, purchase your undergarments at the same time you purchase an outfit, for a perfect polished look. No need to mention panty lines here, right? Or slips? One of my pet peeves is a slip showing underneath a skirt with a slit up the side or back.

1. When you are choosing an outfit for an interview, always dress up, unless you are instructed otherwise by the human resources representative. Dressing up says that you respect the organization and the people you are about to meet. Just because a corporate culture encompasses a "dress down" atmosphere doesn't mean that you should dress that way for an interview or visit to their headquarters. When in doubt, dress up, or ask.

2. Also a note from Mom – buy an iron.

3. If someone compliments you on your dress, simply say, "Thank you" – do not go on and on about the outfit, why you decided to wear it, or – even worse – don't discount it by saying, "This old thing? I haven't worn it in years!" A compliment is like a gift that should be accepted graciously.

4. Fingernails should be well-manicured and not distractingly long.

— *Part Eleven* —

PERSONALLY SPEAKING

Social graces apply both to our business and social lives, even though the events may be different. Whether attending a wedding shower or memorial service, our good manners speak volumes about ourselves and how we view our relationships with others. I wanted to take a moment to review some of these special times in our lives, and challenge you to always remember the other person first. As I have mentioned, etiquette is all about making sure other people are comfortable. The "rules" of manners may have to be broken to accomplish this. If someone eats your salad by mistake, you are not going to shout, "You've eaten my salad!" or embarrass them by telling the server that their salad has been consumed by someone else. You may just have to skip it this time!

> *You must listen to your own heart.*
> *You can't be successful if you aren't happy*
> *with what you're doing. –Curtis Carlson*

Here's what's driving people crazy –

1. The host discusses how much to give the wait staff.

2. My date or host asks me to leave the tip, or asks me how much to leave.

3. People you are dining with don't tip or don't leave enough.

4. My dinner partner is habitually late, leaving me to sit alone.

5. People who have had too much to drink insist on driving.

6. My host does not tell me what to expect; for example, a barbeque or a formal dinner?

7. People do not follow through with their duties at special occasions, such as weddings and memorials.

8. People remove a teacup from the saucer and leave the saucer behind, and slurp!

9. Guests at an afternoon tea ask for teas that are not being offered.

— Chapter 22 —
Remembering the Social Graces

This is a good place to talk about keeping promises, especially when we are attending life-changing events such as weddings, funerals, showers, etc. When emotions are already at an all-time high, make sure that you do what you said you would do. Are you the designated driver after a wedding reception? Then take the lead and make sure everyone knows it and they are safe. Are you the one responsible for moving the flowers from the church to the reception? Then make a plan for a vehicle; don't wait until the last minute and announce that these giant displays won't fit into your Volkswagon bug. If you are in charge of the food at a memorial service in someone's home, coordinate away. The family needs you, and this is your chance to show them how much you care. Here's where your style and grace shines, and is very much appreciated.

DATING

When it comes to dating, nerves may be the only thing you share in common! All of the same etiquette rules we have previously discussed apply, of course, but there's definitely a few unique things to keep in mind!

For example, try to set realistic expectations – otherwise you may be setting yourself up for a big disappointment. Accept the fact that there is value in spending time with another individual, even if it isn't the beginning of a long relationship.

We've talked about the power of a positive attitude and conversation; it also applies to dating. Accept a date with enthusiasm to create excitement for your date. If you must cancel a date, do it as far in advance as possible. Only emergencies should require a last-minute cancellation.

Whether you are picking someone up or meeting them somewhere, be on time. If you must be late, call your date (it's a good idea to share each other's cell phone numbers, just in case). If someone is picking you up, be ready! And, when meeting at a restaurant or whatever, clarify exactly where you will meet. There is nothing more frustrating than waiting in a dining room while your date is sitting in the lobby. FYI – It is considered more polished to meet in the lobby or foyer.

Take special care with your dress and appearance; doing so tells your date that you care about the evening. I once had a friend whose date appeared on her doorstep with an obviously well-worn jacket, only to see that there was a family of tiny spiders crawling around his shoulder! Or how about the person who forgets to remove the price tag from a suit sleeve, or the dress that has dust marks on the shoulder, or – deodorant marks?

Conversation skills are critical to a fun date. And that means LISTENING. As you know, a good conversationalist is a good listener who asks follow-up questions, and doesn't monopolize the conversation with stories about him/herself. Here's a few more things to keep in mind:

1. Your car should be clean, clean, clean, and not smell like yesterday's cheeseburger.

2. Do not flirt with anyone else on the premises, including the servers. I once had a server flirt with my date in a fine restaurant. It caused him embarrassment, and he was forced to speak to her about it while I was away from the table.

3. Keep your conversation positive. No one likes a negative person, especially when you are supposed to be having fun!!! And, do not gossip about others. NEVER complain about the food or drink you are served! If you are hosting the meal, it puts your guest in an awkward position, and really ruins the mood.

4. Don't be a snooty wine expert. I once dined with someone who asked the server what specific temperature they had stored our wine. He replied, "I'm not sure – it is usually opened faster than we can keep refrigerated!" Of course, if you have bad wine, send it back in a gracious way, then refrain from complaining about it the rest of the meal.

5. Whatever you do, don't talk about previous relationships, how much money you make, your last surgery, or how your gout has been acting up.

6. Be careful about touching your date. Similarly to when we discussed hugging, most people do not appreciated being touched, unless and until it is appropriate, probably not on the first date!

7. And, that kiss good-night. We all know it is coming. You be the judge, but remember, there's something very special about a kiss on the cheek after the first date. After all, if you are interested in a second date, it gives you something to look forward to!

ALCOHOL ALERT!

I could write volumes about the stories I have heard, and I'm sure you have some as well. Most people are not at their best when they have over-consumed alcohol, so be very, very careful. Pace yourself and drink water between cocktails or wine to help, but watch it. What do you do if your date has too much to drink? First, try to help them pace by drinking slowly yourself. Also, make sure you order plenty of food – and order it BEFORE you have alcohol. Suggest dessert with coffee, and do not recommend after-dinner drinks. After a meal, suggest a walk around the grounds.

What if the driver has had too much to drink? Hopefully, they would be gracious enough to take your suggestion for a cab. If not, you may need to be more aggressive, and call a cab yourself. No relationship is worth risking your life. Take the lead, and you will probably be thanked for it the next day.

ATTENDING CELEBRATIONS AND FAMILY EVENTS

Whether a wedding or Thanksgiving meal, social events with family and friends provide great opportunities for family fun and personal relationship building. If you think of it this way instead of, perhaps, another "dreaded holiday," you may be surprised.

In my opinion, the biggest mistake people make with regard to these events is treating them too informally. For example, if I'm attending a business function, I'm very careful to mind my manners, greet people and shake hands, etc., but am I as conscious about my manners with my family? You bet!

Let's start with the invitation. Invitations should be extended a few weeks in advance for any event, and you should RSVP as soon as possible. It is next to impossible to plan a meal – especially a meal at your home – without knowing how many people to expect. If you are hosting the meal, make sure to include "and guest" in your invitation (even if you are calling people), to let them know it is okay to bring someone.

With regard to family celebrations, do not assume that the person who had the event last year will have it again. It is a nice idea to offer to this year's hostess that you host the event next year.

As our families grow up and grow out, it may not be possible to observe the traditions you had when your family included yourself, your spouse, and your children. In-laws may now be involved. It's best to discuss how to share the holidays, and be understanding when people can't travel from afar. If you find it is impossible to get your family together during the winter, create your own family event during the summer. The key is to get your time together, whenever that time might be.

Just as in corporate America, strong personalities surface in families. Please don't be that person who is obsessed with having every holiday at your house every year. You know what they say, "If you love someone, let them go," and I believe this is very true when it comes to holidays. Be flexible. If your family can't make it for the actual meal, invite them for cocktails. If they can't come for the actual holiday, invite them for brunch the next day. It is all about getting together!

If you are budget conscious or just like to share recipes, invite your relatives for a potluck! It's nice to ask them what they'd like to bring instead of asking for a particular dish. Then, if they don't have any idea what to bring, be ready with a suggestion.

When attending formal events such as weddings and memorials, be especially mindful of your manners and dress. Emotions are never more sensitive than at these events, so take the lead of the hosts, and try not to upset the applecart. If you have any questions about these events, contact your host well in advance. And, remember not to bring a guest unless you are invited to, and watch your alcohol consumption.

HOUSE GUESTS

Whether for holidays or other special events, let's talk about "house guest" behavior, a sensitive topic for those who have particularly challenging friends and relatives. When staying in someone else's home as a guest, the primary rule is to treat your hosts and their home with great respect. Take a look at these "house rules," and see how you measure up:

1. Bring a host/hostess gift when you arrive such as a bottle of wine, basket of snack goodies, or flower arrangement (not fresh cut flowers – save your host from stopping to arrange flowers when you arrive).

2. Do not bring a pet unless you are invited to do so; even asking if it is "okay" to bring your pet puts your host in an uncomfortable situation. Likewise, please do not bring additional friends or ask if they can come, unless you are encouraged to do so.

3. Be mindful of your surroundings, including your room or open area in which you sleep (make your bed and keep your bathroom tidy and clean). If you are sleeping in a common area, ask your host where they would like you to keep the bedding and your personal effects, and keep your clothing folded neatly and placed out of site.

4. Offer to help with tasks, but not to the point of being annoying! Some hosts like to prepare meals on their own, and don't enjoy sharing their kitchen, while others do. Your job is to offer, then respect their wishes.

5. Be agreeable! Often those who are hosting you have given great thought as to the schedule of meals, etc., and if you can go along with the plan, it will keep things running smoothly.

6. If you are visiting work associates, relax completely by deciding together to leave work talk at the office – out of your conversations. Once this decision is made, you can get to know your friends in a new light, away from work.

7. Leave a thank-you note or gift in your room — your hosts will appreciate the extra thought. It could be something you purchase while out shopping or sightseeing with them, something they admired along the way.

MANAGING AWKWARD MOMENTS

Sometimes things simply go wrong. A piece of meat falls on the floor. Someone forgets someone's name. A ladybug flies into your salad. No matter whether business or pleasure, the best approach is to make whatever problem there is disappear as quickly as possible! And, that means you may be the one to do it.

Generally speaking, it is the responsibility of the host to take care of any mishaps, but in the absence of the host, it is the nearest person. The objective is to make the embarrassment go away and make things as beautiful as possible (especially at the table), and NOT to make jokes about it throughout the evening.

Here's a few examples:

1. If a piece of meat falls on the floor – quietly alert the server. Likewise for a knife or fork. In someone's home, pick it up and take it to the kitchen.

2. If you forget someone's name, simply say your own name and shake their hand. That is usually a tip-off that you need their name as well. If that doesn't work, say something like, "Please help me remember your name." Don't apologize or go on about forgetting their name.

3. If a piece of lettuce falls off your plate, pick it up. If it has dressing on it, leave it.

4. If you've forgotten to turn off your cell phone, do so and apologize for it being on.

5. If someone tells an inappropriate joke, change the subject completely and get away from jokes.

6. If someone slurps soup, stacks their plates, or turns their coffee cup upside down, ignore it all. We can't manage someone else's manners.

7. If the conversation turns nasty or negative, take charge and change the subject!

8. If someone spills something on themselves, offer your clean handkerchief or clean napkin, or escort them away from the table for some help. Sometimes when this happen, panic sets in, and the person can't move!

9. If you spill something on someone, offer the same assistance, and also offer to pay their dry cleaning bill. Follow-up with a phone call or note to make this happen.

By taking charge of awkward moments, you show your leadership as well as your social skills, and you will be remembered for it!

— Chapter 23 —
It's High Time for Afternoon Tea!

Hosting the perfect tea party can be as easy as pie, or, in this case, tea cakes! Let's start with a little clarification. Most people think of "high tea" as the fancy, formal social affairs held in the afternoon. Actually, the term "high tea" refers to a dinner tea held later (around 5-6pm) featuring a heavier menu of meats and cheeses. The dainty tea most of us picture is actually called "afternoon tea," and is held in the mid-afternoon (around 3 or 4pm). This is the event that showcases pastries, tiny finger sandwiches and scones. If you are hosting a tea party, I recommend you refer to it as an "afternoon tea," which implies the lighter menu. It is important for your guests to know what to expect.

The invitations to your afternoon tea should be of quality, and sent via the U.S. mail to set the tone for a stylish event. Not to worry, they can be printed on your computer, purchased, or printed, but should be pretty and individually addressed. To encourage your invitee to bring a friend or associate, please include "and guest" in their invitation (Ms. Sandra Smith and Guest). It is a nice touch to address your invitations using honorifics; i.e., "Mr. and Ms." Assuming your event is a business-related event, do not address a woman by her husband's name; for example, use Ms. Barbara Barclay. (Should you host a social tea, it is appropriate to use husband's name; for example, Mrs. John Barclay.) Feel free to ask for an RSVP.

Set the mood for an "English-style" tea with your fine china and beautiful teacups. It is not necessary for them to match; in fact, some say it is preferred if you have many different types to choose from. A large porcelain or silver teapot is a must. Then collect your best serving trays of all sizes and heights to add interest to the table. And make sure to include small butter knives, teaspoons and fabric napkins as well. A more "American-style" tea would include more of a color theme and matching teacups, etc., so feel free to set your table this way if you are not going for the English-type theme.

The table setting is simple, but deliberate. Place the plates, napkins, butter knives and napkins at one end of the table. Place your centerpiece (flowers or fruit) in the middle of the table, surrounded by your platters of food. Place your teapot, cups and saucers at the other end of the table. Keep a hot water kettle on hand in the kitchen (or a larger urn for bigger parties) to refresh your tea. Tip: consult with your florist about flowers appropriate for a food setting – flowers with a heavy scent can interfere with the aromas of your food.

The tea can be either American or English, but, as your showcase item, should be the best you can afford. While many people enjoy their tea plain, it is important to offer milk, lemon and sugar. Use tea leaves, not bags. Your guests should not have to deal with tea bags!

Serving tea can be done by a tea server (should not be the hostess as she should be welcoming the guests and keeping the conversation going) or your guests may serve themselves. When pouring tea, while some people prefer to pour the milk in first, I suggest adding it last to assure the proper amount. Cream is not served with tea as it is simply too heavy.

Use lemon slices, not wedges, and either supply your guests with small cocktail forks to squeeze the lemon into their cups, or, if there is a server, they may place a slice (using a fork) into the tea after it has been poured.

A variety of sugars and sugar substitutes should be offered.

The food for your English-style afternoon tea should be bite-sized, and include three offerings: finger sandwiches, scones or crumpets with jam and clotted cream, followed by sweets such as petit fours, cookies, small pieces of cake or tarts. Your selection of finger sandwiches could include salmon, egg salad, cream cheese and watercress, chicken and/or tuna salad, tomato, etc. The sandwiches should be cut into different shapes and sizes, and beautifully displayed on your various trays.

An American-style tea would include a sampling of your favorite bite-sized hors d'oeuvres that would combine well with tea, such as mini quiches, possibly biscuits and jam, and pastries and/or chocolate for your sweets.

All food should be easily consumed without a knife and fork, although a knife for spreading a scone with clotted cream is, of course, necessary.

Background music is always nice, and should be classical and very quiet, adding to the atmosphere, not interrupting conversation. The whole idea of your gathering is to provide a wonderful place to enjoy conversation, tea and food.

The role of the hostess is critical to your afternoon tea's success. There's nothing more welcoming than a warm smile and handshake when greeting your guests. It is the hostess's job to assure that all guests are comfortable, both physically and socially. This means that the hostess should take their coats, introduce them to at least one other person or group of people, and direct them to the tea. The hostess should resist the urge to hug guests. In business, a warm handshake is more appreciated and you avoid the awkwardness of possibly hugging one person but not another. If a presentation is to be made, do so once most of the guests have arrived. And, remember to say good-bye to your guests as they leave and thank them for coming.

To properly drink tea . . . pick up your cup and saucer at the same time, holding the saucer in one hand and the cup in the other. Slip your index finger through the handle, and place your thumb on the top of the handle to steady your cup. Please don't extend your pinky finger! Sip your tea while holding the saucer under your cup.

Be careful not to slurp or make clanking noises while stirring your tea. Do not sip from your teaspoon, and rest it on the saucer behind the cup, not inside.

— *Part Twelve* —
POLISHING THE APPLE

As you have seen, while matters of etiquette are primarily common sense, there are many things to keep in mind when meeting and talking with people, whether business or pleasure. I congratulate you on understanding the importance of these social graces, and rest assured that the time you devote to polishing your professional behavior will be rewarded at work and at home.

> *People who don't take risks*
> *generally make about two big mistakes a year.*
>
> *People who do take risks*
> *generally make about two big mistakes a year.*
> *–Peter Drucker*

Here's what's driving people crazy –

1. People refer to men and women as girls and boys.

2. People chew gum in the workplace or when talking on the phone.

3. People make cell phone calls from their cars while visiting drive-thru restaurants.

4. People do not thank others for holding the door open for them.

5. People do not request separate checks, then argue about who owes what.

6. People are unaware that their backpacks or bags are knocking people over!

—— *Chapter 24* ——

A Little Polish Goes a Long Way

There are a few items that bear mentioning when it comes to what's most important: you! It's time to polish the apple, so, here we go:

ABOUT GENDER

Gender makes no difference in business etiquette – the same rules apply for women and men. Be careful not to call women "girls" or men "boys," rather use "women" and "men." Do not refer to groups of people as "you guys." Women shake hands the same as men, introduce themselves standing up just the same as men, etc. However, there are times when women go first, such as through a door.

DOOR OPENING

As mentioned before, it is appropriate for women to open doors for men, although they should give the man a chance at it first. When it comes to car doors, if a female executive picks up a client in her car, it is appropriate for her to open the door the first time the male client gets into the car (or at least walk him to that side of the car), both as a courtesy and to identify which car they will be using. After that, she should go to her side of the car and allow the man to open his own door.

BUSINESS CLOTHING

The rule is professional at all times for both women and men. To be safe, choose conservative clothing and keep it well maintained. I mention this in this section because sometimes women tend to "fashion-up" which sometimes translates to too informal and/or sexy for business attire.

PAYING THE CHECK

The smart female executive can avoid this whole problem by making arrangements in advance – just give your credit card to the server or host before the meal begins! Male guests should not offer to "chip in" or "buy a bottle of wine." Whoever does the inviting pays the bill, the whole bill. If you are dining with your workmates and prefer separate checks, make sure to tell the server ahead of time, rather than taking the time to figure it out at the end – your server will appreciate it!

FLIRTING

The topic is sensitive but it deserves a mention, particularly in our more casual society. Be careful that your friendly demeanor and natural charm does not cross the line of good taste.

The safest way to avoid awkward (and sometimes costly) misunderstandings is simply to keep your business conversations focused on business topics.

If you become uncomfortable because a client starts to "come on" to you or asks you out, don't panic. Thank them, tell them you are flattered by their interest, but just say, "No, thank you." You do not need to offer any further explanation.

This rejection can create a vulnerable moment in the relationship, so to avoid any embarrassment to the other party and to show them you are still interested in them as a business associate, just continue the discussion as if nothing unusual had happened.

KISSING

It bears mentioning to avoid the "air kiss," especially when it comes to business. It tends to appear more in a social arena, and, in fact, is more acceptable there. If you feel an air kiss is appropriate, remember it is the right-hand side of the person's face you will be heading for. Hopefully this tidbit of info will help the experience be a little less awkward!

GUM

If you want to make a good impression – professional or personal – leave the gum at home. And, if you forget, please go to the restroom to dispose of it before drinking a beverage or ordering a meal – or talking on the phone!

PUBLIC DISPLAYS OF AFFECTION (PDA)

Wow, this topic is one that comes up too often for words. Public displays of affection simply make people uncomfortable. Personal behavior such as this should be reserved for private places. With the exception of hand holding, or putting one's arm around someone, one should really refrain from excessive physical affection in public.

ONE MORE THING, CUTIE . . .

If you would like a second appointment with a new client or a second cup of coffee with that special someone, do not call them "honey," "sweetie," or "dear," or "baby." Need I say more?

Thank you!

With this we come to an end for now. I hope you have enjoyed this little book of manners, and invite you to contact me anytime with your questions or comments. And, of course, if you have more examples of, "It drives me crazy when . . ." I'd love to hear them! Thank you, and Cheers!

Informal Setting

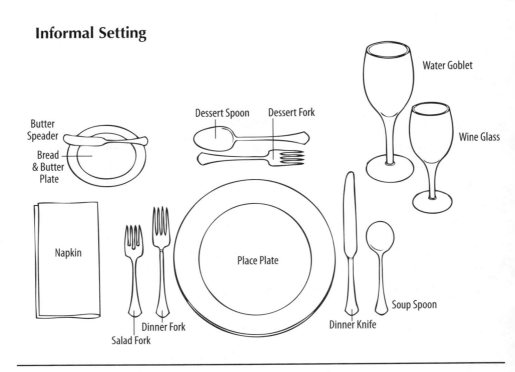

Water Goblet

Wine Glass

Dessert Spoon   Dessert Fork

Butter
Speader
Bread
& Butter
Plate

Napkin

Place Plate

Dinner Knife

Soup Spoon

Dinner Fork
Salad Fork

Formal Setting

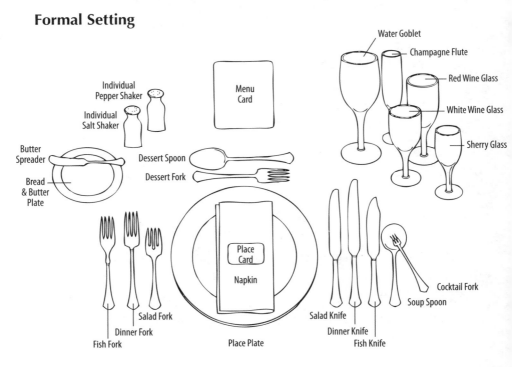

Water Goblet

Champagne Flute

Red Wine Glass

White Wine Glass

Sherry Glass

Menu
Card

Individual
Pepper Shaker

Individual
Salt Shaker

Butter
Spreader
Bread
& Butter
Plate

Dessert Spoon

Dessert Fork

Place
Card

Napkin

Salad Knife

Dinner Knife

Fish Knife

Cocktail Fork

Soup Spoon

Salad Fork
Dinner Fork
Fish Fork

Place Plate

156

— Appendix —
HOW TO EAT CERTAIN FOODS

Here's what's driving people crazy –

1. My tablemate uses his/her teeth to crack crab or lobster.

2. People do not use a knife with a salad, and stuff their mouths with giant pieces of lettuce.

3. People take huge bites of food, then struggle to chew and swallow.

4. Someone offers me bites of their food, and won't take "no thank you" for an answer.

5. People cut up all of the food on their plate, then mix it together and cover it with ketchup or gravy.

If you avoid ordering difficult-to-eat foods such as spaghetti or artichokes, you should be comfortable in any dining situation. However, there are certain basic foods that we face on a regular basis that bear mentioning. Here are some of my favorites:

Bread, rolls and butter

Your bread and butter plate will be the one to the left of your place setting. Bread should be buttered one piece at a time over the bread plate and consumed one piece at a time. Do not butter your bread over your dinner plate or in the air! The exception is breakfast muffins, toast and bagels where you may butter an entire half at one time. Butter balls or pats should be placed on the butter plate with the small fork provided. If there is no serving fork, use your dinner knife, then place the knife on the butter plate after use.

Bananas

Believe it or not, at the dining table, bananas should be peeled, then eaten with a knife and fork. Away from the table, peel it down as you eat.

Bacon

Very crisp bacon may be eaten with your fingers; otherwise, use a knife and fork.

Bones

You may bring the bones of small birds (such as quail) and frog legs to your mouth with your hand.

Caviar

Spread caviar on toast with a knife, then eat with your fingers.

Cocktail fruit

If it is served on a toothpick, feel free to eat it that way. Set the toothpick on a cocktail napkin unless a serving saucer is provided. Don't eat the fruit floating in a cocktail – it is too messy!

Corn on the cob

Don't order it! If it is served to you, do not butter the whole ear at once. Take sections at a time.

Escargot

If the escargot are served in the shell, hold the shell with the tongs and remove the meat with a seafood fork. If they are served in individual cups, eat each one (whole) with the seafood fork. And yes, it is permissible to dip pieces of bread into the sauce!

French fries

Strange as it may feel, you should eat fries with a knife and fork, unless you are dining with your family at a fast food restaurant!

Lemon wedges

Have you ever been squirted in the eye? Hold and squeeze a lemon wedge with your right hand while shielding it from your dining partners with your left. If a fork is available, pick it up with the fork and squeeze out the juice with your other hand. If it is a slice, steady it on your plate with a fork, then squeeze the juice out with a knife.

Lobster and crab

If the lobster is not already cracked, do so with the nutcracker provided. Use your seafood fork to eat the meat. Some people dip it in butter or sauce. Large pieces can be cut with your fork. Eat crab the same way with the exception of soft-shell crabs which are consumed with a knife and fork, shell and all.

Oysters, mussels and clams

Simply hold the shell with one hand and remove the meat with a seafood fork. Dip and enjoy! Sometimes, mollusks can also be taken directly from the shell.

Pasta

The preferred way to eat spaghetti or pasta is to pull aside a few strands at a time and wind them around your fork. In more casual settings, you may use a pasta spoon. Wind the pasta around your fork with the tines in the bowl of the spoon.

Baked potato

Take butter from your bread and butter plate with your dinner knife. You might mash your potato flat at home, but don't do it in public! Yes, you may eat the skin – with your knife and fork.

Relishes, jams and condiments

Place these directly onto your bread and butter plate or dinner plate using the serving spoon provided and use your butter knife or dinner knife to spread.

Salad

Salad is usually eaten with a fork. A salad knife should be provided, if necessary. If not, use your dinner knife. The server should bring you another one, not ask you to keep it for the main meal!

Sandwiches

It is acceptable to eat most sandwiches with the fingers. However, always eat open-faced sandwiches with a knife and fork.

Sauces

Pour or spoon sauces over or beside the meat, where you may dip each forkful into the sauce.

Seeds

Quietly and discreetly expel seeds into your cupped hand or fingers, then set them on the side of your plate.

Shrimp

Eat small shrimp with a seafood fork. Large shrimp can be eaten with the fingers or, if possible, placed on a serving plate and cut with a fork. Hold the shrimp by the tail and dip it into the sauce. Set the tail on the serving plate when you are finished.

Strawberries

Eat sliced strawberries with a spoon. Hold whole strawberries by the stem and eat them in small bites. Set the stem on the side of the plate.

Water

There is even a proper way to drink water! Blot your mouth with a napkin, then take a small sip. Do not drink while food is in your mouth or take huge gulps. Also, do not drain a full glass at one time!